READING GROUP CHOICES
2011

Selections for lively book discussions

READING
GROUP
Choices

Published in the United States by Reading Group Choices,
a division of Connxsys LLC

ISBN 978-0-9759742-6-1

For further information, contact:
Barbara Drummond Mead
Reading Group Choices
532 Cross Creek Court
Chester, MD 21619
Toll-free: 1-866-643-6883
info@ReadingGroupChoices.com
www.ReadingGroupChoices.com

welcome to
READING GROUP *Choices*

Reading is a way of life. Connecting is a way of life. Sharing ideas is a way of life. Reading groups combine all three! Being in a reading group enhances the way you examine books, your life, and the world around you.

Reading Group Choices selects discussible books that will do just that, but will lead to other activities (friendship, support, and a little wine, food, music, another book) that will boost your life experience. In the 2011 edition, you will find many literary choices: mystery, memoir, historical fiction, current affairs, humor, fantasy, and literary fiction. We hope you will find our suggestions helpful to further your literary and world understanding.

Cheers to the trifecta that is a reading group—Good Books, Good Friends, Good Conversation!

And, thanks for keeping the joy of reading alive.

—BARBARA AND CHARLIE MEAD

Book Group Favorites

Early in 2010, we asked thousands of book groups to tell us what books they read and discussed during the previous year that they enjoyed most. The top ten titles were:

1. **The Help** by Kathryn Stockett (Putnam Adult)
2. **The Guernsey Literary and Potato Peel Pie Society** by Mary Ann Shaffer and Annie Barrows (Dial Press)
3. **Loving Frank** by Nancy Horan (Ballantine Books)
4. **The Book Thief** by Markus Zusak (Knopf Books for Young Readers)
5. **Olive Kitteridge** by Elizabeth Stout (Random House Trade Paperbacks)
6. *TIE:* **Still Alice** by Lisa Genova (Pocket Books)
   Sarah's Key by Tatiana de Rosnay (St. Martin's Griffin)
7. **People of the Book** by Geraldine Brooks (Penguin Books)
8. **Three Cups of Tea** by Greg Mortenson & David Oliver Relin (Penguin Books)
9. **The Shack** by William P. Young (Windblown Media)
10. **The Art of Racing in the Rain** by Garth Stein (Harper Paperbacks)

Contents

GUIDELINES FOR
Lively Book Discussions

Respect space—Avoid "crosstalk" or talking over others.

Allow space—Some of us are more outgoing and others more reserved. If you've had a chance to talk, allow others time to offer their thoughts as well.

Be open—Keep an open mind, learn from others, and acknowledge there are differences in opinion. That's what makes it interesting!

Offer new thoughts—Try not to repeat what others have said, but offer a new perspective.

Stay on the topic—Contribute to the flow of conversation by holding your comments to the topic of the book, keeping any personal references to an appropriate minimum.

Come find, friend, and follow us

On the web: **www.ReadingGroupChoices.com**

On our blog: **http://blog.ReadingGroupChoices.com**

On Facebook: **Reading Group Choices Fan Page**

On Twitter: **@ReadingGChoices**

CONVERSATION STARTERS
General ideas to stimulate your book group discussion.

Discuss factual questions and recap the story:

- Who are the key characters?

- Does one or more characters tell the story? How does this affect the narrative?

- Are they believable characters?

- How do their experiences cause them to grow?

- What are the themes?

- What are the conflicts in the story?

- How does the setting and time period affect the story?

Discuss how the story relates to your life:

- How would you react to the same situations?

- Have any of the events in the story happened in your life?

- If a historical story, what would be the advantages/ disadvantages of living in that period? Would you like it? Why? What if it's a science fiction story?

- Look at the jacket. Is it one you would have chosen for this book? Why or why not?

- Did the story change your opinion of a place, event, time period, etc.? How so?

- What do you think will happen to the characters next?

- If the story is made into a movie, whom would you pick to play the characters?

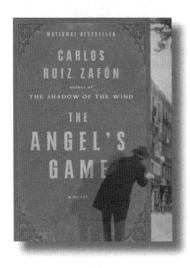

THE ANGEL'S GAME

AUTHOR: *Carlos Ruiz Zafón*

PUBLISHER: Anchor Books, 2009

WEBSITE: www.ReadingGroupCenter.com
www.theangelsgame.net

AVAILABLE IN: Trade Paperback
544 pages, $15.95, ISBN 978-0767931113

ALSO AVAILABLE AS: eBook and Audiobook

SUBJECTS: Love/Intrigue/Literature
(Fiction)

"[Zafón's] visionary storytelling prowess is a genre unto itself."
—*USA Today*

"A dark tale of literary intrigue." —Newsweek

SUMMARY: In this powerful, labyrinthian thriller, David Martín is a pulp fiction writer struggling to stay afloat. Holed up in a haunting abandoned mansion in the heart of Barcelona, he furiously taps out story after story, becoming increasingly desperate and frustrated. Thus, when he is approached by a mysterious publisher offering a book deal that seems almost too good to be real, David leaps at the chance. But as he begins the work, and after a visit to the Cemetery of Forgotten Books, he realizes that there is a connection between his book and the shadows that surround his dilapidated home and that the publisher may be hiding a few troubling secrets of his own. Once again, Ruiz Zafón takes us into a dark, gothic Barcelona and creates a breathtaking tale of intrigue, romance, and tragedy.

ABOUT THE AUTHOR: **Carlos Ruiz Zafón**, author of *The Shadow of the Wind* and other novels, is one of the world's most read and best-loved writers. His work has been translated into more than forty languages and published around the world, garnering numerous international prizes and reaching millions of readers. He divides his time between Barcelona and Los Angeles.

CONVERSATION STARTERS

1. The novel begins with David's recollection of the first time he tasted "the sweet poison of vanity" by writing for a living. How much of his career is fueled by vanity versus poverty? Why was it so difficult for him to heed Cristina's warnings about selling out to greedy publishers?

2. Like Carlos Ruiz Zafón's previous novel, *The Angel's Game* is written in the first person. What does David reveal about his view of the world as he tells us his story? How might the novel have unfolded if it had been told from Andreas Corelli's point of view?

3. Sempere influenced David's life by giving him a copy of *Great Expectations*. Later returned to him by Corelli, the book still bore the bloody fingerprints of David's father. How did David's life resemble a Dickens novel? How was he affected by his parents' history? How did books and booksellers save him? What is the most memorable book you received as a child?

4. What is the common thread in each of Corelli's tactics for luring David? How did you interpret his "dream" of Chloé? What made David a vulnerable target?

5. How does Pedro Vidal justify his exploitation of David, stealing the woman he loves and capitalizing on David's prowess as a writer? How did your opinion of Vidal shift throughout the novel? Does he redeem himself in chapter 22 (act three)? Describe someone whom you idolized early in your career who later proved to be untrustworthy.

6. Explore the novel's title. Ultimately, who are the angels in David's world? What are the rules of Corelli's game? Who are its winners?

7. What is the effect of reading a novel about a novelist? What truths about the intersection of art and commerce are reflected in the story of Barrido & Escobillas and in their subsequent demise at the hands of an even more controlling publisher?

8. How did you interpret the novel's closing scene, particularly the presence of Cristina? Throughout the novel, how did David reconcile the ideal of Cristina with the realities of circumstance?

9. What is special about the bond between David and Isabella? What do they teach each other about love? If you have read *The Shadow of the Wind*, discuss your reactions to Daniel's heritage, revealed in the epilogue.

BEAR SPEAKS
The Story of 7 Sacred Lessons Learned from a Montana Grizzly

AUTHOR: *Laura Carpini*

PUBLISHER: Weiser Books, 2010

WEBSITE: www.redwheelweiser.com

AVAILABLE IN: Trade Paperback
160 pages, $14.95, ISBN 978-1578634828

ALSO AVAILABLE AS: eBook

SUBJECTS: Animals/Family/
Personal Discovery (Fiction)

"Bear Speaks *captivates the mind and teaches us to uncover the truth of Joy in modern life. I wholeheartedly recommend it.*" —**Erich Schiffmann, author of** *Yoga: The Spirit and Practice of Moving into Stillness*

SUMMARY: A young professional woman from Los Angeles goes camping in the Montana wilderness to "find herself" and escape the pressures of family and fiancé, about whom she's having some doubts. As she explores the natural world around her, she encounters the trickster coyote, a wise old spider and an adventurous raven, all of whom have the ability to shapeshift and communicate with her, mind to mind. And soon she finds herself falling in love with a magnificent bear named Ishmel.

As she gets to know Ishmel, he transmits to her seven sacred lessons: All your needs will be met; Time is an illusion; Have no fear; Release into love; Create a loving reality; Connect energy lines to heal the world; Vibrate with joy.

Above all she learns, and teaches us, that the source of your fear can become the guide for your life. *Bear Speaks* tells an enchanted tale about trusting what life presents us.

ABOUT THE AUTHOR: **Laura Carpini** graduated magna cum laude in English literature from UCLA. After a brief and disastrous career as an attorney, she became a middle school teacher. In addition to this book, she has written several screenplays. She is a yogi active in the Santa Monica yoga community.

CONVERSATION STARTERS

1. The protagonist has a wobbly relationship with her father. To what extent does he influence her, and provide her with the skills that allow her to expand her perception of the world in the forest? What is the general role of family in the story?

2. The main character's initial reason for going to the forest is to prove her independence. Yet from the beginning she is reliant on Jerry, handyman and forest ranger extraordinaire. How are her interactions with him a precursor for discoveries about herself and independence that she makes later in the story?

3. How does the appearance of the Coyote become a turning point in the woman's interactions with the forest? Why does her relationship with him help her to settle into her environment?

4. Discuss the earthquake and Ishmel's entrance. How does her initial perception of the Bear as a "stalker" contribute to her fear and excitement when they finally make contact? Discuss the significance of the name Ishmel. What does the Bear's name reveal about what she will learn from him?

5. The woman finds herself drawn to both the Grizzly and Brian. What is the basis for her attraction to Brian, and how does it differ from her need for Ishmel?

6. What are some of the elements of shamanism in the story? To what extent does the main character become a shaman herself?

7. What is the lesson of the Woman in the Cave? Why does the woman warn the protagonist about Ishmel? Are those warnings legitimate?

8. What does the protagonist learn about the role fear plays in her development? How does confronting her fear help her evolve as an individual, and ultimately allow her to become part of a community?

9. Discuss the two rainstorms in the story and the main character's reactions to them. How do the Snake's movements in the second storm coincide with her internal opening? How does that internal change allow her to refashion the external appearance of the forest?

10. Discuss the protagonist's pregnancy and how it connects with Ishmel's teaching about immortality and the ongoing nature of life?

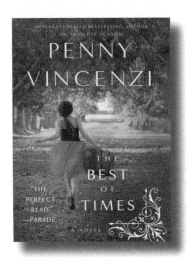

THE BEST OF TIMES

AUTHOR: *Penny Vincenzi*

PUBLISHER: Anchor Books, 2010

WEBSITE: www.ReadingGroupCenter.com
www.pennyvincenzi.com

AVAILABLE IN: Trade Paperback
608 pages, $15.00, ISBN 978-0767930857

ALSO AVAILABLE AS: eBook

SUBJECTS: Relationships/Women's Lives/
Identity (Fiction)

"A perfect read." —**Parade**

"Nobody writes smart, page-turning commercial women's fiction like Vincenzi." —**USA Today**

SUMMARY: On an ordinary Friday afternoon, on a major motorway outside of London, a trailer truck suddenly and violently swerves across fives lanes of traffic—careening cars into one another like dominoes and leaving a trail of chaos and confusion. Within the space of a minute, an astounding miles-long pileup has amassed, and, as the survivors await help, their stories unfold.

Vincenzi expertly maneuvers the plot between the panic-stricken husband trapped in his car with his young mistress, his adultery sure to be discovered; the bridegroom trying frantically to get to the church on time (he won't); the widow on her way to reunite with the love of her life after sixty years, now forced to ponder whether she'll ever see him again; the junior doctor waiting to receive the crash victims in the ER … And at the epicenter of this field of destruction lies the truck driver, suffering from memory loss, while the mysterious hitchhiker, the only person who knows what really happened, has fled the scene.

ABOUT THE AUTHOR: **Penny Vincenzi** is the author of several novels, including *No Angel, Something Dangerous,* and *Into Temptation.* Before becoming a novelist, she worked as a journalist for *Vogue, Tatler,* and *Cosmopolitan.* She lives in London.

CONVERSATION STARTERS

1. The role of chance in our lives is a major theme in this novel. Given the outcomes of the accident for the main characters, how do you interpret the difference between chance and fate in the book? Do you believe in fate?

2. The accident is the pivotal moment in the plot when the characters' lives collide and are changed forever for better or worse. In that moment, which character did you find yourself sympathizing with most and why? Do you have any real anecdotes about traumatic life-altering moments that you'd like to share?

3. In the beginning, many of the characters such as Jonathan, Toby, and Abi are portrayed as morally ambiguous. Which characters did you find most difficult to categorize and why? Did anyone surprise you by how they changed in the aftermath of the crash?

4. In many ways, the accident is just as traumatic for those characters who were not on the M4. Did you sympathize with any of them more than with the crash victims?

5. Everyone makes mistakes sometimes, and terrible mistakes play a large role in this novel. When Daisy gets hit by a car, did you agree with how Jonathan responds to his son Charlie's guilty confession? Do you think it is fair to blame a person for something he/she could never have predicted? Do you think the treatment of the issue of blame is handled well in the novel?

6. Were you surprised that Georgia fled the scene of the accident? Did this storyline successfully add an element of mystery to the plot for you?

7. An allusion to the famous first line of Charles Dickens' *A Tale of Two Cities,* the title of this novel could be interpreted as ironic. Do you think some of the characters' lives were ultimately changed for the better? Was this realistic to you? Do you believe that something good always comes out of something bad?

8. The final part of the novel is entitled "Moving On". Were you convinced that each character successfully moved on? Were you unsure how any of the relationships would fare in the future? If so, which one?

9. *The Best of Times* is Penny Vincenzi's sixth novel published in the United States. Have you read any of Penny's previous books? If so, how does this one compare?

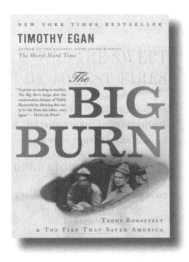

THE BIG BURN
Teddy Roosevelt and the Fire that Saved America

AUTHOR: *Timothy Egan*

PUBLISHER: Mariner Books, 2010

WEBSITE: www.marinerbooks.com
www.timothyegan.com

AVAILABLE IN: Trade Paperback
352 pages, $15.95 ISBN 978-0547394602

ALSO AVAILABLE AS: eBook and Audiobook

SUBJECTS: American History/Biography/
Environment & Nature (Fiction)

"Egan tells the story with great humanity.... In prose so sizzling it crackles, The Big Burn *keeps alive the conservation dreams of Teddy Roosevelt by allowing this story to rise from the ashes, once again."* —**Denver Post**

SUMMARY: On the afternoon of August 20, 1910, a battering ram of wind moved through the drought-stricken national forests of Washington, Idaho, and Montana, whipping the hundreds of small blazes burning across the forest floor into a roasting inferno that jumped from treetop to ridge as it raged, destroying towns and timber in the blink of an eye. Forest rangers had assembled nearly ten thousand men—soldiers, college boys, day workers, immigrants from mining camps—to fight the fire. But no living person had seen anything like those flames, and neither the rangers nor anyone else knew how to subdue them. In this epic story of an America outgrowing its manifest destiny, Timothy Egan narrates the struggles of the overmatched rangers against the implacable fire while also drawing a dramatic portrait of president Teddy Roosevelt and his chief forester, Gifford Pinchot.

ABOUT THE AUTHOR: **Timothy Egan** is a Pulitzer Prize-winning reporter and the author of five books, most recently *The Worst Hard Time*, which won a National Book Award for nonfiction, and was named a *New York Times* Editors' Choice and a *New York Times* Notable Book. He writes a weekly column, *"Outposts,"* for the *New York Times*.

CONVERSATION STARTERS

1. This gripping account begins with the fire's destruction of Wallace, Idaho. What kinds of things make people late to the evacuating train? What would you bring with you if you were allowed only a case small enough to fit on your lap?

2. Egan details the childhood and early careers of both Teddy Roosevelt and Gifford Pinchot in order to give readers a fuller picture of why and how these men came to pioneer conservation as a national value in America. In what ways do Roosevelt's experiences shape his politics? How do Pinchot's experiences influence his work as "Big G.P." of the Forest Service?

3. Roosevelt and Pinchot are very different types of men, and yet they share a passion for the great outdoors. What do Roosevelt and Pinchot have in common? How are they different from one another?

4. Throughout the book, Egan reveals that some powerful men whose hubris and greed would decide the fate of America's still-untamed West spend time in that region, while others distance themselves both literally and figuratively. Discuss the relationship these men have to the land they all but rule over and the way Egan portrays them.

5. Gifford Pinchot firmly believed that man could control forest fires, though he'd never seen anything like the Big Burn of 1910 when he published his *A Primer of Forestry* in 1900. What methods do the rangers and townsfolk use to try to control the fires? What methods do they use to survive?

6. The aftermath of the Big Burn seems like one colossal governmental failure, though some bright spots exist, such as the sea change in many Americans' opinions about the black "buffalo soldiers" who became heroes in Wallace, Idaho. How does Egan's portrayal of this seminal moment in American history make you feel? Did it change your mind about anything, or teach you anything new?

7. William H. Taft is portrayed as a complicated man in this book. He idolizes Roosevelt and yet fails to keep his promises to him; on page 246, Egan describes how he publicly attacks T.R. in an effort to save face, but retreats afterward to weep in private. Do you feel any sympathy for Taft? Why or why not?

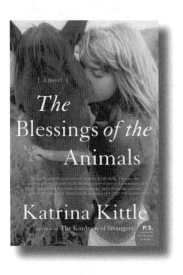

THE BLESSINGS OF THE ANIMALS

AUTHOR: *Katrina Kittle*

PUBLISHER: Harper Perennial, 2010

WEBSITE: www.harperperennial.com
www.katrinakittle.com

AVAILABLE IN: Trade Paperback
464 pages, $14.99, ISBN 978-0061906077

ALSO AVAILABLE AS: eBook

SUBJECTS: Animals/Personal Challenges/
Relationships (Fiction)

"[A] beautifully crafted novel. . . . A must-read not only for animal lovers, but for anyone who has found the courage to come back from heartbreak and find love again, without reservation, without fear." —**Sara Gruen, *New York Times* bestselling author of *Water for Elephants***

SUMMARY: Veterinarian Cami Anderson has hit a rough patch. Stymied by her recent divorce, she wonders if there are secret ingredients to a happy, long-lasting marriage or if the entire institution is outdated and obsolete. Her parents are preparing to celebrate their fiftieth anniversary. Her brother and his partner find their marriage dreams legally blocked. Her former sister-in-law—still her best friend—is newly engaged. The youthfully exuberant romance of her teenage daughter is developing complications. And three separate men—including her ex-husband—are becoming entangled in Cami's messy post-marital love life.

But as she struggles to come to terms with her own doubts amid this chaotic circus of relationships, Cami finds strange comfort in an unexpected confidant: an angry, unpredictable horse in her care. With the help of her equine soul mate, she begins to make sense of marriage's great mysteries—and its disconnects.

ABOUT THE AUTHOR: **Katrina Kittle** is the author of *Two Truths and a Lie* and *The Kindness of Strangers*. She lives in Dayton, Ohio, where she teaches English and theatre at the Miami Valley School.

CONVERSATION STARTERS

1. The last line of Chapter Two has Cami entering the house (where Bobby will leave her), remembering the time she tried to touch a tornado. She thinks, "How could I have been so certain I wouldn't be hurt?" How does the tornado story parallel marriage?

2. How does the Bobby chapter affect your reading of the story? Without his point of view, what would be different for you? What does he think that you wish he'd tell Cami? What things do both Bobby and Cami misinterpret in each others' actions?

3. Discuss the importance of the scarred Passier saddle in light of what Cami learns about her parents' marriage.

4. Why is it so important for Cami to ask Bobby if he wants to work on the marriage? Would you have done the same thing? Or is this another example of her not knowing when to quit?

5. Why is it important for Cami to reclaim "Bobby's" kitchen? How does Muriel help with this decision?

6. What *are* the blessings of the animals? What gift does each of the three main animals (Moonshot, Gerald, and Muriel) give to Cami? How do these rescue animals end up rescuing her? What final gift or lesson does Luna bring at the end?

7. In what ways do the Davids epitomize the marriage vows they are not allowed to make?

8. Discuss Cami's reaction to Vijay's proposal. Are her concerns justified? Is she making a mistake?

9. Cami comes to believe that Bobby gave her a gift the day he walked out. Do you agree or disagree?

10. Cami and Vijay love each other but Vijay says, "And that's not enough." Is he right? Is this a true assessment when considering forming a life together?

11. After the disastrous wedding shower for Olive, what "advice" would you offer to newlyweds?

12. Is Cami right to think "What a risk love was." How do you feel about her final thoughts, "We were all—every one of us—rushing out into the hail. Dancing out into the hail every single day"? What does she mean?

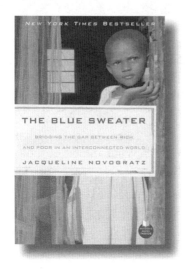

THE BLUE SWEATER
Bridging the Gap Between Rich and Poor in an Interconnected World

AUTHOR: *Jacqueline Novogratz*

PUBLISHER: Rodale, 2010

WEBSITE: community.acumenfund.org/page/
the-blue-sweater

AVAILABLE IN: Trade Paperback
320 pages, $15.99, ISBN 978-1605294766

ALSO AVAILABLE AS: eBook

SUBJECTS: Social Issues/Women's Lives/
Culture & World Issues/(Memoir)

"An empowering, heartfelt portrait of humanitarianism at work."
—*Kirkus* (starred review)

"A visionary book . . . devoted to providing opportunity to poor people in all countries in an interconnected world." —Deepak Chopra, *San Francisco*

SUMMARY: Jacqueline Novogratz left a career in international banking to spend her life on a quest to understand global poverty and find powerful new ways of tackling it. From her first stumbling efforts as a young idealist venturing forth in Africa to the creation of the trailblazing organization she runs today, Novogratz tells gripping stories with unforgettable characters. She shows, in ways both hilarious and heartbreaking, how traditional charity often fails, but how a new form of philanthropic investing called *patient capital* can help make people self-sufficient and can change millions of lives. More than just an autobiography or a how-to guide to addressing poverty, *The Blue Sweater* is a call to action that challenges us to grant dignity to the poor and to rethink our engagement with the world.

ABOUT THE AUTHOR: **Jacqueline Novogratz** is founder and CEO of Acumen Fund, a nonprofit venture capital firm for the poor that invests in sustainable enterprises.

CONVERSATION STARTERS

1. Do you have any experiences like Jacqueline's blue sweater story that explore the same types of themes in your life?

2. One theme is the importance and power of listening to others. What are some examples from the book of either failure to listen or success in listening? Can you think of some instances from your own life where listening more or less might have changed an outcome?

3. Jacqueline sees moral imagination as the ability to put yourself in someone else's shoes and see the world from their perspective. When is moral imagination most necessary? How is it related to the concept of dignity? Is it a skill that can be taught?

4. What caused the women's initial distrust of Jacqueline when she first arrived in Kenya? How does one build trust? How can trust be rebuilt after great tragedies like the Rwandan genocide or in countries where corruption might be the norm?

5. Why do you think Jacqueline wanted to return to Rwanda after the genocide? What did she learn from her conversations with Honorata, Liliane, Agnes, and Prudence during her return trips? How did these stories of change Jacqueline's understanding of human nature or your understanding of human nature?

6. Jacqueline encounters failure many times throughout her life. Think about how her failures shaped future decisions. What is the relationship between failure and success?

7. What is the difference between seeing the poor as customers and seeing them as receivers of charity as with WaterHealth International in Chapter 15? Should poor people have to pay for basic services like water and housing?

8. Discuss the philosophy behind the instrument of patient *capital,* which Jacqueline describes in Chapter 13. Does this seem like a viable solution to solving the problems of poverty? What other instruments exist for poverty alleviation?

9. Do you agree with how Jacqueline went about changing the bakery in Nyamirambo and the lives of the women who worked there? What effects did it have? How were Jacqueline's efforts with the bakery different from the patient capital approaches she later espouses?

10. Despite her focus on building businesses to solve poverty, Jacqueline gives money directly to the poor at various points in the book. Why does she give the money away? Has this book changed how you might donate your money in the future?

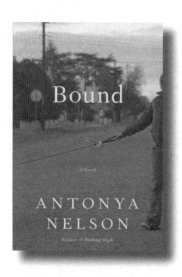

BOUND

Author: *Antonya Nelson*

Publisher: Bloomsbury USA, October 2010

Website: www.bloomsburyusa.com

Available in: Hardcover
240 pages, $25.00, ISBN 978-1596915756

Also Available as: eBook

Subjects: Relationships/Family/Mystery (Fiction)

"Nelson's prose looks to be as sleekly tough-minded as ever . . . essential for those serious about contemporary literature." —Library Journal

Summary: Even after nearly two decades of marriage, Oliver and Catherine Desplaines maintain their secrets. Oliver, an aging entrepreneur, has spent his life looking for the next opportunity, in business and love. Catherine is his third wife, closer in age to his estranged daughters, and he's just fallen giddily, yet again, for an even younger woman.

Catherine herself is seemingly placid and content, supporting Oliver's career and heaping affection on their pet corgis, but she has ghosts of a past she scarcely remembers. When her high school best friend dies, Catherine learns she is the namesake, and now guardian, of a missing teenage girl. Another specter of her adolescence has also risen: the notorious serial killer, BTK (Bind, Torture, and Kill), taunting Wichita police and boosting local news ratings after years of silence.

About the Author: **Antonya Nelson** is the author of nine books of fiction, including *Nothing Right* and the novels *Talking in Bed*, *Nobody's Girl*, and *Living to Tell*. Nelson's work has appeared in the *New Yorker*, *Esquire*, *Harper's*, *Redbook*, and many other magazines, as well as in anthologies such as *Prize Stories: The O. Henry Awards* and *The Best American Short Stories*. She has received a Guggenheim Fellowship, an NEA Grant, the Rea Award for the Short Story, and, recently, the United States Artists Simon Fellowship. She is married to the writer Robert Boswell and lives in New Mexico, Colorado, and Texas, where she holds the Cullen Chair in Creative Writing at the University of Houston.

CONVERSATION STARTERS

1. *Bound* begins and ends with Max, Misty and Cattie's dog who survives a car crash and finds a new life in Arizona. What does Max's dog's-eye view add to the novel? How are Cattie, Randall, Catherine, and Elise changed by dog ownership over the course of the novel?

2. Misty dies in the first chapter of *Bound*, but her life becomes clearer as the novel continues. What first impression does Misty make before her fatal car accident? How does Misty's character come into focus, as we learn more about her early years in Wichita and her midlife successes in Houston?

3. Discuss how Cattie handles the loss of her mother. How does she manage her grief, and at which moments is she overwhelmed with emotion? Consider the feelings of guilt that Cattie expresses when she declares, "the fact remained: her mother had been alive, and sober, when they lived in the same place" (30).

4. Oliver and the BTK are both "Wichitans to Watch" in the local newspaper. How does Oliver react to this public link to the serial killer? Why does Oliver feel a private "shiver of troubling recognition" when the BTK is finally caught (223)? Which of his own secrets does Oliver recognize within the BTK's rise and fall?

5. Catherine eventually realizes that Cattie "had not been running away, she'd been running home" (191). What does "home" mean to Catherine and to Cattie? Does either of them find a true home by the end of the novel? Why or why not?

6. Discuss the second-to-last scene of *Bound*, Yasmin Keene's funeral. How does the ceremony bring characters together in new ways? Why does Catherine confess to Dr. Keene's children, "Your mom terrified me," instead of simply reading her mother's prepared list of Dr. Keene's accomplishments (209)? Why do Dr. Harding and Oliver both disapprove of Catherine's emotional words? How does Cattie cope with attending a funeral that is not her mother's?

7. Consider the significance of names in the novel. Why might Misty have named her daughter after her old friend Catherine? What does a dog's change in name—from Misty's "Max" to Elise's "Prozac"—suggest about the power of naming in *Bound*?

8. Discuss the meaning of the title *Bound*. Who is bound together in the novel—legally, emotionally, or unwillingly? Which bonds are broken over the course of the novel, and what new bonds are formed?

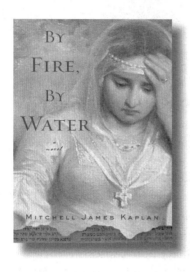

BY FIRE, BY WATER

AUTHOR: *Mitchell James Kaplan*

PUBLISHER: Other Press, 2010

WEBSITE: www.otherpress.com
www.mitchelljameskaplan.com

AVAILABLE IN: Trade Paperback
320 pages, $15.95, ISBN 978-1590513521

ALSO AVAILABLE AS: eBook and Audiobook

SUBJECTS: Religion/Intrigue/Identity
(Historical Fiction)

"Debut novelist Kaplan depicts a turbulent period in 15th-century Spain, focusing on the story of Aragon's royal chancellor. . . . Deftly moves through a complex web of personal relationships, religious zeal and political fervor." —**Kirkus Reviews**

SUMMARY: Luis de Santángel, chancellor to the court and longtime friend of the lusty King Ferdinand, has had enough of the Spanish Inquisition. As the power of Inquisitor General Tomás de Torquemada grows, so does the brutality of the Spanish church and the suspicion and paranoia it inspires. When a dear friend's demise brings the violence close to home, Santángel is enraged and takes retribution into his own hands. But he is from a family of conversos, and his Jewish heritage makes him an easy target. As Santángel witnesses the horrific persecution of his loved ones, he begins slowly to reconnect with the Jewish faith his family left behind. Feeding his curiosity about his past is his growing love for Judith Migdal, a clever and beautiful Jewish woman navigating the mounting tensions in Granada. While he struggles to decide what his reputation is worth and what he can sacrifice, one man offers him a chance he thought he'd lost . . . the chance to hope for a better world. Christopher Columbus has plans to discover a route to paradise, and only Luis de Santángel can help him.

ABOUT THE AUTHOR: **Mitchell James Kaplan** has lived and worked primarily in Paris and Los Angeles as a translator, screenwriter, and script consultant.

CONVERSATION STARTERS

1. What did you know about the Spanish Inquisition (1478–1834) prior to reading *By Fire, By Water*? How did this story influence or increase your understanding of this historical period?

2. In *By Fire, By Water*, trusting someone can lead to life or death. Discuss the various relationships in the novel that lead to both. What kind of trust do the characters have in God? How does trust vary depending on the character's social class or religious beliefs?

3. How do the female characters, living in a strongly patriarchal society, acquiesce to or rebel against their culture's expectations of them? How does Judith break the mold for female behavior in her community? What about Judith catches Santángel's eye, and later compels him to seek her out?

4. What compels Santángel to learn about the Jewish faith? What is each group member's purpose for joining his secret religious meetings? How does the small group help, support, or hurt its members?

5. Discuss the significance of the novel's title, *By Fire, By Water*.

6. Why do you think Leonor, Felipe's wife, feels so protective of Santángel when he is the one who allowed Felipe to join the secret group, and thus, is partially to blame for her husband's death?

7. On page 97, Judith loses Levi for an afternoon and, in her search and worrying, reassures herself that, "History never repeats itself." Do you find evidence in the novel to support this claim?

8. What was your impression of King Fernando and Queen Ysabel? How do the monarchs differ from Granada's emir? What do they have in common?

9. What influence do religious leaders hold over the king and queen? How does this influence differ from that of Santángel and his money? Do you think any religious leaders have that sort of power today?

10. How did the author's depiction of Cristóbal Colón contradict or conflict with your own personal knowledge of Christopher Columbus, who famously discovered the New World in 1492?

11. Why is Colón so keen to push his foreign documents on Santángel? Do you believe their friendship was authentic, or was Colón merely interested in exploiting Santángel's influence on the king and queen?

12. Discuss the meaning of exile in the novel and how various characters experience it both literally and metaphorically.

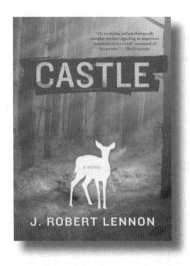

CASTLE

AUTHOR: *J. Robert Lennon*

PUBLISHER: Graywolf Press, 2010

WEBSITE: www.graywolfpress.org
www.jrobertlennon.com

AVAILABLE IN: Trade Paperback
240 pages, $14.00, ISBN 978-1555975593

ALSO AVAILABLE AS: eBook and Audiobook

SUBJECTS: Family/Social Issues/Mystery
(Fiction)

"A brilliant, classical, psychological horror story that sticks to and gnaws at the bones." —*Oregonian* **(Portland)**

SUMMARY: "In the late winter of 2006, I returned to my home town and bought 612 acres of land on the far western edge of the county." So begins, innocently enough, J. Robert Lennon's gripping and brilliant new novel. Awkward, guarded, and more than a little adamant about his need for privacy, Eric Loesch sets about renovating a rundown old house in the small, upstate New York town where he spent his childhood. When he inspects the title to the property, however, he discovers that there is a plot of dense forest smack in the middle of his land that he does not own. What's more, the name of the person it belongs to is blacked out. Loesch sets out to explore the forbidding and almost impenetrable forest. But this peculiar adventure story has much to do with America's current military misadventures—and Loesch's secrets come to mirror the American psyche in a paranoid age. The answer to what—and who—might lie at the heart of Loesch's property stands at the center of this daring and riveting novel.

ABOUT THE AUTHOR: **J. Robert Lennon** is the author of four novels including *Mailman* and *The Light of Falling Stars*. His stories have appeared in, the *Paris Review, Granta, Playboy, Harper's*, and the *New Yorker*. He lives in Ithaca, New York, with his wife and two sons.

CONVERSATION STARTERS

1. Eric Loesch evades the questions he is asked by the Gerrysburg townspeople, and at times he even grows belligerent in response to their prodding. The reader does not initially know why he is keeping his distance from them or what he is being defensive about—what effect does this have on your perception of the protagonist?

2. How much do the townspeople know about Loesch, his family history, and his war experience? How does this information affect their behavior toward him, and what does their behavior suggest about the American public's attitude toward its returning veterans?

3. Loesch is asked by three different characters—the real estate agent, his sister, and finally Professor Stiles—why he has returned to Gerrysburg before he poses the question himself toward the novel's end. Do you believe Loesch when he claims that he "didn't believe that [he'd] ever known" the reason he decided to return home?

4. For the first two-thirds of *Castle*, Loesch does not explain the significance of objects from his childhood or the landscape he once inhabited—the locomotive, the rock outcrop, the castle, and his toys —and yet he conveys to the reader his strong emotional responses to these things. When Loesch first finds the castle, he reports, "It was as though something hanging crookedly in my mind had finally been righted." What does Loesch remember? Is this a case of repressed memory or something else?

5. J. Robert Lennon describes the woods as a place beset by a dark history, almost as though it were haunted. And then there is the mysterious castle at its center. Is this a realistic novel or an allegory? What is the castle's metaphoric significance?

6. Discuss the relationship between young Loesch and Doctor Stiles. Why does Loesch turn away from his father and toward the strict disciplinarian Stiles?

7. Why does Loesch's father seem intent on having his son "trained" by the professor? What does he feel is lacking in his son, and in the broader culture of that time?

8. As Loesch leaves for his next mission at the novel's end, he says, "I took a last look around the house, pleased at the work I had done, pleased at everything I had learned since my return to Gerrysburg." What has Loesch learned from his time in Gerrysburg?

CHEAP CABERNET
A Friendship

AUTHOR: *Cathie Beck*

PUBLISHER: Voice, 2010

WEBSITE: www.everywomansvoice.com
www.cathiebeck.com

AVAILABLE IN: Trade Paperback
336 pages, $14.99, ISBN 978-1401341541

ALSO AVAILABLE AS: eBook

SUBJECTS: Women's Lives/Relationships/
Inspiration (Memoir)

"Beyond wonderful—wickedly funny, poignant, and smart. Anyone who's a fan of Mary Karr or Anne Lamott will find Cathie Beck's Cheap Cabernet *both laugh-out-loud hysterical—and heartbreaking."* —**Elle Newmark, bestselling author of *The Book of Unholy Mischief***

SUMMARY: Cathie Beck was in her late thirties and finally able to exhale after a lifetime of just trying to get by. A teenage mother harboring vivid memories of her own hardscrabble childhood, Cathie had spent years doing whatever it took to give her children the stability—or at least the illusion of it—that she'd never had. More than that, through sheer will and determination, she had educated them and herself too. With her kids in college, Cathie was at last ready to have some fun. The only problem was that she had no idea how to do it and no friends to do it with. So she put an ad in the paper for a made-up women's group: WOW . . . Women on the Way. Eight women showed up that first night, and out of that group a friendship formed, one of those meteoric, passionate, stand-by-you friendships that come around once in a lifetime and change you forever . . . if you're lucky.

ABOUT THE AUTHOR: **Cathie Beck** is a Denver-based journalist and creative writer who has been, at various times, a baton-twirling teacher, a cocktail waitress, a secretary, and a writing teacher. This is her first book.

CONVERSATION STARTERS

1. Why does Cathie feel the need to start a women's group? What crossroads has she arrived at in her life? How does her children moving away from home change the way she feels about her place in society?

2. Cathie and Denise become fast friends, but their relationship is far from smooth, even at the beginning. In what ways do their personalities clash? In what ways do they complement one another? Why do you think their complex relationship ends up being so special?

3. Why does Cathie retell the story of applying for food stamps when her children are young? What does that story tell the reader about Cathie's life as a young mother? What do we learn about her background, and how does it inform the woman we meet in the memoir?

4. Denise and John have unique and unconventional marriage. How does Cathie feel about their relationship? Do you think she envies them, or pities them? What about the marriage works for Denise, and in what ways does the arrangement fail her? Do you think John and Denise are in love? Why or why not?

5. Cathie had very complicated, mixed feelings about Denise's illness. In what ways does Cathie let Denise's MS affect their friendship? Would you say that Cathie takes care of Denise when she is ill? In what ways does Denise's MS frustrate and disappoint Cathie?

6. Discuss Cathie and Denise's trip to Jamaica and Cuba. In what ways is the trip a turning point for both women? What do they each discover about themselves on the trip and what do they discover about one another?

7. Toward the end of the memoir, Cathie writes about her own mother and the struggles she faced raising Cathie and her siblings. Is Cathie anything like her mother? In what ways does Cathie escape her families' legacy? In what ways does she continue where her mother left off? How does her family and her childhood haunt her into her adult life?

8. In the end, Cathie and Denise have a falling out and Cathie does not attend her friend's memorial service. Do you think Denise orchestrated their rift to protect Cathie, as Cathie assumes? Do you think Cathie can really find closure?

9. *Cheap Cabernet* follows in a tradition of many great memoirs, novels, and movies about women's friendships. How does this book fit in to that tradition? How is Cathie and Denise's friendship unique from others you have read about or seen?

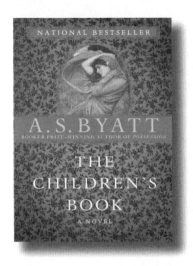

THE CHILDREN'S BOOK

AUTHOR: *A. S. Byatt*

PUBLISHER: Vintage Books, 2010

WEBSITE: www.ReadingGroupCenter.com

AVAILABLE IN: Trade Paperback
896 pages, $16.95, ISBN 978-0307473066

ALSO AVAILABLE AS: eBook and Audiobook

SUBJECTS: Family/History/Relationships
(Fiction)

Shortlisted for the Man Booker Prize

Majestic. . . .Dazzling. . . .Wonderful. . . .What you see here. . . Is the strength and fire of Byatt's imagination." —**The San Francisco Chronicle**

SUMMARY: When Olive Wellwood's oldest son discovers a runaway named Philip sketching in the basement of the new Victoria and Albert Museum— a talented working-class boy who could be a character out of one of Olive's magical tales—she takes him into the storybook world of her family and friends.

But the joyful bacchanals Olive hosts at her rambling country house—and the separate, private books she writes for each of her seven children— conceal more treachery and darkness than Philip has ever imagined. As these lives—of adults and children alike—unfold, lies are revealed, hearts are broken, and the damaging truth about the Wellwoods slowly emerges. But their personal struggles, their hidden desires, will soon be eclipsed by far greater forces, as the tides turn across Europe and a golden era comes to an end.

ABOUT THE AUTHOR: **A. S. Byatt** is the author of numerous novels, including the quartet *The Virgin in the Garden, Still Life, Babel Tower*, and *A Whistling Woman; The Biographer's Tale*; and *Possession*, which was awarded the Booker Prize. She has also written two novellas, published together as *Angels & Insects*; five collections of shorter works, including *The Matisse Stories* and *Little Black Book of Stories*; and several works of nonfiction.

CONVERSATION STARTERS

1. Why is this novel called *The Children's Book*? Discuss the many possible meanings this title suggests.

2. A German puppeteer is a surprise guest at the Wellwoods' Midsummer party at the beginning of the novel. What role do puppets play in the novel, and what do they represent? How does the relationship between the German and British characters change as the novel unfolds?

3. What is the significance of the Tree House? What does it mean to Tom—and to his siblings?

4. Motherhood is a crucial part of the novel, and of Olive's stories; Olive herself is something of a "Mother Goose," as in her story "The Shrubbery". But is Olive a good mother? What about Violet, and the other mothers in the story?

5. A number of the adult characters are artists in one way or another; many of them—through their art or their actions—cause damage to the other people in their lives. Discuss how the artists in the novel both create and destroy.

6. Discuss the Fludd family. Why do you think Byatt chose not to divulge the specifics of Benedict's acts? What do you think he did?

7. How is Dorothy—who doesn't share her mother's love of stories, who is the serious daughter, and who becomes a doctor—different from her siblings? How does Humphry's revelation, and his betrayal, change her?

8. What is the significance of the stone with a hole that Tom picks up?

9. Why does Hedda try to destroy the Gloucester Candlestick? Is it a coincidence that she chose this item? How does the suffragette movement affect her and the other women in the story?

10. *The Children's Book* is a historical panorama that encompasses many political and social movements of the early twentieth century. Were you familiar with the figures and movements Byatt discusses: the Fabian Society, British socialists, women's rights, etc.? What is your understanding of their purpose in the novel?

11. The acknowledgments give a glimpse of the research that went into the novel; what subjects did you most enjoy learning about? How does Byatt's erudition enrich her storytelling?

12. Reread pages 878–879, the last pages of the novel. Is it a happy ending? What emotions are conjured by this reunion, which takes place in a far different setting than that which opens the novel—and around a bowl of soup?

CLEO
The Cat Who Mended a Family

AUTHOR: *Helen Brown*

PUBLISHER: Citadel Press Trade Paperback, 2010

WEBSITE: www.kensingtonbooks.com
www.helenbrown.com.au

AVAILABLE IN: Trade Paperback
304 pages, $15.95, ISBN 978-0806533032

ALSO AVAILABLE AS: eBook

SUBJECTS: Family/Inspiration/Biography (Nonfiction)

"The next Marley & Me. *Even non cat-lovers will be moved."*
—*Good Housekeeping*

SUMMARY: "We're just going to look." Helen Brown had no intention of adopting a pet when she brought her sons, Sam and Rob, to visit a friend's new kittens. But the runt of the litter was irresistible, with her overlarge ears and dainty chin.

When Cleo was delivered weeks later, she had no way of knowing that her new family had just been hit by a tragedy. Helen was sure she couldn't keep her—until she saw something she thought had vanished from the earth forever: her son's smile. The reckless, rambunctious kitten stayed.

Through happiness and heartbreak, changes and new beginnings, Cleo turned out to be the unlikely glue that affectionately held Helen's family together. Rich in wisdom, wit, heart, and healing, here is the story of a cat with an extraordinary gift for knowing just where she was needed most.

ABOUT THE AUTHOR: **Helen Brown** was born and brought up in New Zealand, where she first worked as a journalist, TV presenter, and scriptwriter. *Cleo* rose to the top of the bestseller list in its first weeks in the United Kingdom, New Zealand, and Australia.

CONVERSATION STARTERS

1. What would you say are the main themes of *Cleo*?
2. Which characters do you identify with most? Faced with similar tragedy do you think you would behave differently?
3. Has the book changed how you might behave towards someone experiencing grief? If so in what ways?
4. Cleo had an enormous impact on her grieving family. Discuss the importance of pets in an age of technology and splintering families. Has an animal changed your life in any way?
5. Helen claims not to be a cat person, partly because of her semi rural upbringing. Are "cat people" and "dog people" born or created? How would you describe yourself?
6. Conventional religion is not a source of comfort for Helen. How important is spirituality in this story? Is it a major factor in your own life?
7. For much of the book Helen struggles with forgiveness. How is it possible to truly forgive someone who has been responsible for the death of your child?
8. In what ways is losing a child different from losing a partner or parent?
9. Why is there tension in Helen and Steve's relationship, even before the tragedy? Do you think they should have worked harder to make their marriage work?
10. Helen embarks on a relationship with Philip, a much younger man. Would you describe her as a typical Cougar? Why do you think there's a spotlight on older women/younger men relationships?
11. Discuss Rob and his journey into adulthood. Does the loss of his older brother Sam enrich him in any way?
12. Which character do you think helps the family most? "Bubbles, darling?" Ginny; Rosie who knows everything about cats; Arthur Judson who waited at the accident scene or somebody else? Discuss everyday heroes, and the ones you have met.
13. Cleo teaches Rob and Helen to smile again. How appropriate is light heartedness in midst of tragedy?
14. Despite advances in grief counselling many people are unwilling to talk openly about death, the death of children in particular. Would society be healthier if dying was regarded as a necessary part of living?
15. Was Cleo special, or do all pets have the capacity to improve people's lives?

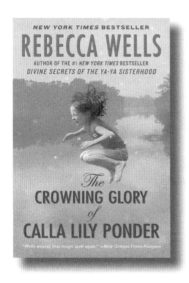

THE CROWNING GLORY OF CALLA LILY PONDER

AUTHOR: *Rebecca Wells*

PUBLISHER: Harper Paperbacks, 2010

WEBSITE: www.rebeccawellsbooks.com
www.harpercollins.com

AVAILABLE IN: Trade Paperback
416 pages, $13.99, ISBN 978-0060930622

ALSO AVAILABLE AS: eBook

SUBJECTS: Family/Identity/Relationships
(Fiction)

"The Crowning Glory of Calla Lily Ponder *will remind you of your first love and power of friendship. As the saying goes, 'You'll laugh, you'll cry.' But, really, you will."* —**Real Simple**

"Calla Lily Ponder *is every bit as affable as her name suggests. . . . Expect high demand from loyal* Ya-Yas *fans, who have eagerly awaited a new work from Wells."* —**Booklist**

SUMMARY: When small town Louisiana girl Calla Lily Ponder encounters sweet, sexy, succulent love on the banks of the La Luna River, she thinks her future with Tuck LeBlanc is a given. But when he disappears into the Ivy League world which she will never be a part of, she must make her own way. Using the gifts of healing, which her mother gave her, Calla leaves the familiarity of her hometown and heads to the untamed city of New Orleans, where love and adventure and beauty school help her magical destiny unfold.

A shining new stand-alone novel from #1 *New York Times* bestselling *Ya-Ya* author Rebecca Wells illuminates the pull of first love, the power of life, and the human heart's capacity for healing.

ABOUT THE AUTHOR: **Rebecca Wells** is the author of *New York Times* bestsellers *Ya-Yas in Bloom, Little Altars Everywhere*, and *Divine Secrets of the Ya-Ya Sisterhood*, which was made into a feature film. A native of Louisiana, she now lives on an island in the Pacific Northwest.

CONVERSATION STARTERS

1. Wells lives in Seattle now, but Louisiana is clearly still vivid in her life and work. Talk about Wells' fictional Louisiana, and how the setting of La Luna expands that growing landscape.

2. The natural world plays a major role in this story: the La Luna River and the Moon Lady are as fully realized and important as any of the human characters. Talk about how Wells is able to weave together the mystical and the ordinary. Why do you think this works?

3. *The Crowning Glory of Calla Lily Ponder* is a stand-alone novel, in which Rebecca Wells introduces a brand new character, Calla Lily Ponder. Wells has referred to this new book as a "spiritual cousin" to her Ya-Ya books. How do you think it relates to Wells' previous works?

4. Wells' previous books have dealt extensively with the idea of sisterhood. This new novel depicts female friendships across racial, generational, and socio-economic lines. Talk about Calla's "sisters," and how each one provides different kinds of support for her emotional journey.

5. Wells has observed that in mythology, legend, and even in present time, hair symbolizes the soul. Hair plays a large role in Calla's life. What does "crowning glory" mean in this story? Why is it such a touchstone for Calla throughout her life, especially when paired with her memories of her childhood? What does the book's title signify to you?

6. Think about some of the unbreakable bonds Calla has in her life: with M'Dear, with Sukie. Talk about the Moon Lady's influence as a guiding force throughout Calla's life. Is it just as strong or even stronger than Calla's human relationships?

7. Over the course of the book, Calla experiences first love and then, later, a more mature love. How do the men in her life reflect both her essential nature and her growth? Talk about Wells' ability to depict male characters in this story.

8. Calla goes through heartbreak and loss throughout this story, but she manages to find inspiration through tragedy. How is she able to do this? Is this a strength she was born with?

9. What do you imagine might happen between Calla Lily and Tuck the day/week/month after they drink that cup of coffee together?

Find more discussion questions, visit www.harpercollins.com/readers

CROWN OF DUST

AUTHOR: *Mary Volmer*

PUBLISHER: Soho Press, November 2010

WEBSITE: www.sohopress.com
www.maryvolmer.com

AVAILABLE IN: Hardcover
292 pages, $24.00, ISBN 978-1569478615

ALSO AVAILABLE AS: eBook

SUBJECTS: American History/Intrigue/
Relationships (Fiction)

"Carefully researched and meticulously imagined. Volmer has written a new story of the California gold rush that is as believable and transporting as any I have ever read. The town of Motherlode—a collection of misfits, exiles, and escapees—having weathered the trials of isolation, of claims that don't pan, of families left behind and dreams disappointed, is about to get civilized. Volmer's characters are wonderful and the story is tense and engaging. A wonderful read."—**Karen Joy Fowler, author of** *The Jane Austen Book Club* **and** *Sister Noon*

SUMMARY: The Gold Rush has taken hold of the Wild West. Pioneers from around the country congregate in makeshift settlements like Motherlode in hopes of striking it rich. It's here that Alex, disguised as a boy and on the run from her troubled past, is able to blend in among the rough and tumble prospectors living on little more than adrenaline and moonshine.

Word spreads quickly when Alex becomes the first in Motherlode to strike gold. Outsiders pour in from wealthy east coast cities, primed to cash in on the discovery. But these opportunitsts from the outside world have no place in Motherlode and threaten to rip the town—and its residents—apart. Alex must fight to protect her buried secrets—and her life.

ABOUT THE AUTHOR: **Mary Volmer** was born in Grass Valley, California, and now lives in the San Francisco Bay Area. She earned a Masters degree from the University of Wales, Aberystwyth, as a Rotary Ambassadorial Scholar and an MFA in Creative Writing from Saint Mary's College, California. This is her first novel.

CONVERSATION STARTERS

1. Although Alex is the most notable example, most of characters in *Crown of Dust* are in some way haunted by, and running from, their pasts. Do any of these characters succeed in escaping their pasts?

2. "Some men," says Emaline, "Some men just need killing." Do you believe Alex's crime was justified? If she ever meets Jackson Hudson again, would she be justified in killing him? Do you think she would kill him?

3. Discuss the unique social order in place in Motherlode when Alex arrives. Who governs the place? How are disputes settled? How are poplar 19th century notions of religion, spirituality and morality revised to fit the needs of this community?

4. In what way is Emaline's authority, and the town itself, threatened by the discovery of gold and by the quick arrival of "polite" society? Is this threat adequately illustrated by the conflict between Emaline and Mrs. Dourity? Are women, like Mrs. Dourity, to blame for perpetuating rigid gender roles in society? What attitudes and fears motivate Emaline and Mrs. Dourity's mutual disregard?

5. "She no longer minds the fatigue, the rough calluses forming on her hands, the solid indentions developing where she never dreamt muscles lurked. With each new ache, she discovers a new, living part of herself. Filling out, the men call it, but to Alex it feels more like filling in..."

6. While Alex cannot physically become a boy, hard physical labor in the mine does transform her body and her mind. Describe how this transformation changes her perspective of her own worth and of her place in the town. How does this transformation change how others view her?

7. If David had not discovered Alex was a woman, do you think he would still have allowed himself to love her?

8. In spite of her love for Jed, Emaline's treatment of the Chinese miners reveals she is not free of racial prejudice. Do her actions disappoint you? Why does she feel justified in mistreating the Chinese men? What does her behavior reveal about the complicated nature of racial prejudice?

9. Before reading *Crown of Dust*, what did you know about the California Gold Rush? How did this novel shape your understanding of the daily life, the prevalent biases, prejudices and hardships prospectors endured during the Gold Rush? Were you aware of the role women played in shaping new gold rush communities?

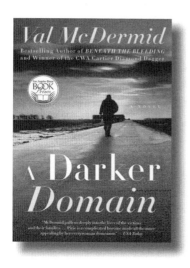

A DARKER DOMAIN

AUTHOR: *Val McDermid*

PUBLISHER: Harper Paperbacks, 2010

WEBSITE: www.valmcdermid.com
www.harpercollins.com

AVAILABLE IN: Trade Paperback
368 pages, $14.99, ISBN 978-0061688997

ALSO AVAILABLE AS: eBook

SUBJECTS: Mystery/Social Issues/History (Fiction)

"A Darker Domain *combines a thrilling story with heartbreaking questions of social justice and history.*" —*Seattle Times*

"*McDermid pulls us deeply into the lives of the victims and their families. . . . Pirie is a complicated heroine made all the more appealing by her everywoman demeanor.*" —*USA Today*

SUMMARY: *Fife, Scotland, 1984.* Mick Prentice abandons his family at the height of a politically charged national miners' strike to join the strikebreakers down south. Despised and disowned by friends and relatives, he is not reported missing until twenty-three years later.

Fife, Scotland, 1985. Kidnapped heiress Catriona Maclennan Grant is killed and her baby son vanishes when the ransom payoff goes horribly wrong. In 2008, a tourist in Tuscany stumbles upon dramatic new evidence that reopens the investigation.

Already immersed in the Prentice affair, Detective Karen Pirie, newly appointed head of the Cold Case Review Team, wants to make her mark with this second unsolved 1980s mystery. But two decades' worth of secrets are leading Pirie into a dark domain of violence and betrayal—a place darker than any she has previously entered.

ABOUT THE AUTHOR: Scottish crime writer **Val McDermid** is the author of twenty-three novels. Her books have won the Gold Dagger Award for Best Crime Novel of the Year and the *Los Angeles Times* Book Prize, been named *New York Times* Notable Books, and been nominated for the Edgar Award. She lives in the north of England.

CONVERSATION STARTERS

1. The investigation into Mick Prentice's disappearance is opened after his daughter, Misha, attempts to track down living family as a bone marrow match for her son. Would you seek out a family member who had abandoned you in order to help your child? Would you take it to the police in the way that Misha brought her search?

2. The 1984 miners' strike in Scotland was a landmark dispute in the United Kingdom. The resulting poverty for the miners and their families was often extreme. How does the strike affect the relationships described throughout the book, whether it is ties between family or friends?

3. Do you sympathize with the miners that left Scotland for work in England? Do you feel the stigma attached to the wives and children left behind by those that did flee was unfair? Would you have stayed behind and waited out the strike, which would eventually come to an end after a year?

4. Did Jimmy Lawson's retelling of the night of the hand-off in the Maclennan Grant case affect your opinion of Sir Broderick or Catriona or the circumstances of the kidnapping?

5. Why do you think Catriona's mother had such a hard time handing the bag to Catriona that night?

6. Knowing what he did about the circumstances of the kidnapping and the death of his mother, did you expect Gabriel / Adam to seek out his grandfather?

Find more discussion questions, visit www.harpercollins.com/readers

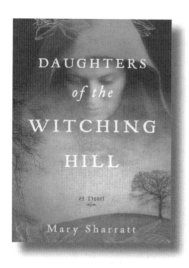

DAUGHTERS OF THE WITCHING HILL

AUTHOR: *Mary Sharratt*

PUBLISHER: Houghton Mifflin Harcourt, 2010

WEBSITE: www.houghtonmifflinbooks.com
www.marysharratt.com

AVAILABLE IN: Hardcover
352 pages, $24.00, ISBN 978-0547069678

ALSO AVAILABLE AS: eBook

SUBJECTS: History/Intrigue/Family
(Fiction)

A fascinating tale. The story unfolds without melodrama and is therefore all the more powerful. Recommended for fans of Katherine Howe's The Physick Book of Deliverance Dane." —**Jamie Kallio**, *Library Journal*

SUMMARY: Bess Southerns, an impoverished widow living in Pendle Forest, is haunted by visions and gains a reputation as a cunning woman. Drawing on the Catholic folk magic of her youth, Bess heals the sick and foretells the future. As she ages, she instructs her granddaughter, Alizon, in her craft, as well as her best friend, who ultimately turns to dark magic. When a peddler suffers a stroke after exchanging harsh words with Alizon, a local magistrate eager to make his name as a witch finder plays neighbors and family members against one another until suspicion and paranoia reach frenzied heights.

ABOUT THE AUTHOR: **Mary Sharratt** is an American writer living in the Pendle region of Lancashire, Northern England. Her new novel *Daughters of the Witching Hill* tells the vivid and wrenching story of a family caught in the Pendle witch-hunt of 1612. Her inspiration for the book arose directly from the wild, brooding landscape: the true story of the Pendle Witches unfolded almost literally in her backyard.

The author of the critically acclaimed novels *Summit Avenue*, *The Real Minerva*, and *The Vanishing Point*, Sharratt is also co-editor of the subversive fiction anthology *Bitch Lit*, a celebration of female antiheroes, strong women who break all the rules.

CONVERSATION STARTERS

1. What did you learn about life in northern England during this time?

2. Comparing the Pendle Witch Trials to the more familiar Salem Witch Trials of 1692, what primary differences crop up in the social forces driving the two witch hunts?

3. Does book's portrayal of magic and cunning folk in Early Modern Britain feel authentic to you? Did the book change any of your views on historical witchcraft?

4. Unlike many other accused witches in historical trials, Bess freely admitted to being a cunning woman, and she even bragged to the magistrate about her familiar spirit, Tibb, who appeared to her in the guise of a beautiful young man. Why didn't Bess try to save herself by denying the accusations?

5. Who, or what, is Tibb, Bess's familiar spirit? Do you see him as good, evil, or neutral? Does he ultimately benefit Bess or lead her into tragedy?

6. The cunning craft Bess practiced reveals a sincere faith in the power of Catholic prayer charms combined with folk beliefs in familiar spirits, sympathetic magic, and the Fairy Folk. Would you describe her worldview as ultimately Christian or Pagan? How does Bess's spiritual vision differ from that of her fellow accused witch, Alice Nutter, a recusant Catholic, who concealed outlawed priests in her manor house?

7. After Bess instructs her best friend, Chattox, on the craft, Chattox turns to dark magic. Is Chattox justified in harnessing dark powers to protect her daughter, Anne Redfearn, from rape when she knows the authorities will do nothing to help her? What would you have done in Chattox's situation?

8. What do you think is the origin of the "green sickness" that kills Alizon's best friend, Nancy? How did the view of illness in this period mirror beliefs in witchcraft and the supernatural?

9. Alizon's brother, Jamie, suffers from learning difficulties. Outside the circle of his loving family, people call him an idiot and treat him callously. How does his affliction shape his fate?

10. What do you think of magistrate Roger Nowell and his actions? Why is he so obsessed with witch-hunting? After having known about Bess and her magical activities for several decades, why does he wait until 1612 to make his move?

11. What enduring message does the Pendle Witch Tragedy have for people of our time?

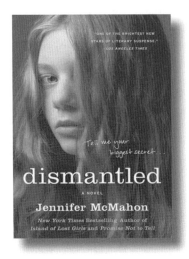

DISMANTLED

Author: *Jennifer McMahon*

Publisher: Harper Paperbacks, 2010

Website: www.jennifer-mcmahon.com
www.harpercollins.com

Available in: Trade Paperback
432 pages, $13.99, ISBN 978-0061689345

Also Available as: eBook and Audiobook

Subjects: Mystery/Coming of Age/
Identity (Fiction)

"An eerie and gripping tale of suspense. . . . A triumph."
—Boston Globe

Summary: When Henry, Tess, Winnie, and Suz form the Compassionate Dismantlers in college, the first rule of their manifesto is, "To understand the nature of a thing, it must be taken apart." But their penchant for acts of meaningful vandalism and elaborate, often dangerous pranks results in Suz's death in the woods of Vermont—a tragedy the surviving Dismantlers decide to cover up.

Nearly a decade later, Henry and Tess are desperate to forget, but their guilt isn't ready to let them go. When a mysterious Dismantler-style postcard drives a past prank victim to suicide, it sets off a chain of terrifying events that threatens to tear apart their world and engulf their inquisitive nine-year-old daughter, Emma. Is there someone who wants to reveal their secrets? Or is it possible Suz has found a way to enact revenge?

Full of white-knuckle tension with deeply human characters caught in circumstances beyond their control, Jennifer McMahon's enthralling story proves that she is a master at weaving the fear of the supernatural with the stark realities of life.

About the Author: **Jennifer McMahon** is the author of *Island of Lost Girls* and *Promise Not to Tell*. She lives in Vermont with her partner, Drea, and their daughter, Zella.

CONVERSATION STARTERS

1. In *Dismantled*, identity is a fluid concept: Val is transformed into Winnie, Winnie poses as Suz, Suz questions her identity as leader of the Dismantlers, Danner is never quite who she seems to be. How much of our identity is influenced by outward appearances, and by how others perceive us? How easy is it to reinvent yourself?

2. The Compassionate Dismantlers believe that by following their manifesto, they can transform art, themselves, and ultimately society. When relatively harmless pranks evolve into more destructive acts, the members have to decide where to draw the line. How far would you go in the name of something you believed passionately?

3. Emma's quirks and obsessions drive much of the action in the present day narrative of *Dismantled*. Do you think her idiosyncrasies are a reaction to something in her upbringing?

4. *Dismantled* is told from multiple points of view. Did you think this technique was effective? Did you trust certain points of view more than others?

5. As a reader, you come to know Suz both through others' memories of her and through her diary. Is Suz a sympathetic character? Is she misunderstood or misguided? Do you see her as a hero or villain?

6. Throughout the novel, Henry and Tess must reevaluate their marriage and their feelings for each other. Much of their current state is dictated by their past. Do you think it's possible to overcome past hurts and reestablish the love in a relationship? How do you think the set-up of Henry living in his studio affects Emma?

7. Tess finds outlets from the stresses of her life through boxing and through art. Winnie suggests to Emma that she also find a creative outlet through art. How important do you think it is for people to find a place or activity they can go to forget about the world around them? Are there things you do to combat stress in your life?

8. Much of the action is set off by the characters' need to feel a sense of belonging: Spencer desperately wants to be a dismantler, Winnie wants to be loved by Suz, Henry wants to be back with his family, and Emma is looking for a friend who understands her. How does their need to be a part of something dictate how they act? Would you classify them as outsiders?

Find more discussion questions, visit www.harpercollins.com/readers

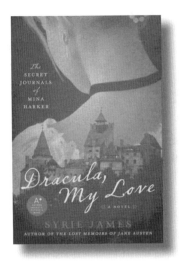

DRACULA, MY LOVE
The Secret Journals of Mina Harker

AUTHOR: *Syrie James*

PUBLISHER: Avon A, 2010

WEBSITE: www.syriejames.com
www.harpercollins.com

AVAILABLE IN: Trade Paperback
480 pages, $14.99, ISBN 978-0061923036

ALSO AVAILABLE AS: eBook

SUBJECTS: Love & Romance/Relationships/
Women's Lives (Historical Fiction)

"With its poetic, 19th-century prose style, this tale about a fierce, forbidden romance will appeal to even the most jaded romance fan."
—**Library Journal**

SUMMARY: Syrie James approaches Bram Stoker's classic *Dracula* with a breathtaking new perspective—as, for the first time, Mina Harker records the story of her scandalous seduction and sexual rebirth.

Who is this young, magnetic, handsome, fascinating man? And how could one woman fall so completely under his spell?

Struggling to hang on to the deep, pure love she's found within her marriage, Mina Harker is inexorably drawn into a secret, passionate affair with a charismatic but dangerous lover. This haunted and haunting creature has awakened feelings and desires within her that she has never before known, which remake her as a woman.

Although everyone she knows is pledged to destroy Count Dracula, Mina sees a side to him that others cannot: a tender, romantic side; a man who's taken advantage of his gift of immortality to expand his mind and talents; a man who may not be evil after all. Soon, they are connected in a way she never thought humanly possible. Yet to surrender is surely madness, for to be with him could end her life.

ABOUT THE AUTHOR: **Syrie James** is the bestselling author of *The Lost Memoirs of Jane Austen* and *The Secret Diaries of Charlotte Brontë*. She's been hailed as "the queen of nineteenth century re-imaginings" by *Los Angeles Magazine*. An admitted Anglophile, Syrie lives in Los Angeles. She welcomes visitors and messages at www.syriejames.com

CONVERSATION STARTERS

1. Who are your favorite characters in *Dracula, My Love*, and why? Who is your least favorite character? How is Count Dracula similar to or different from the Dracula portrayed in Bram Stoker's novel, and/or in any of the film versions you've seen?

2. Compare and contrast the characters of Lucy and Mina in *Dracula, My Love*. How do the differences between them ultimately affect their fates?

3. Discuss Mina's character arc. At the beginning of the story, what are her viewpoints regarding love, marriage, a woman's role in society, and the need to follow that society's rules? Is Mina an example of traditional Victorian mores? How does Mina grow and change over the course of the story?

4. Early in the novel, Mina admits that she's always told Lucy everything, and that she and Jonathan made a solemn pact to be completely honest with each other. Yet Mina conceals her relationship with Mr. Wagner/Dracula from both Lucy and Jonathan. Why? How does the burden of carrying that secret affect her and influence the choices she makes?

5. Discuss the scenes which explore the truth of Mina's parentage and personal history. How does her back story add to her character and to the novel as a whole? How does Mina and Jonathan's shared history influence their present and future?

6. Discuss Dracula's origin story as revealed in the novel. How did his personal misfortunes shape the being he becomes? Do you admire him for the choices he's made? Why or why not?

7. If you had an eternity before you, how would you spend it?

8. Mina reminds Jonathan that her dreams often come true. Did this fact affect your expectations while reading the novel? How does Mina's dream imagery serve the story? When Mina dreams that Dracula makes love to her, do you think it was really just a dream?

9. Did reading Mina's story in the first person enhance the experience for you? What are the benefits and limitations of telling a story from the main character's perspective, rather than the third person?

10. Discuss the book's climax and resolution. Do you think the ending was appropriate? What caused Dracula to react and behave the way he did? At the final moment, do you think he did the right thing?

11. Examine the final paragraph of the novel. In what ways has Mina's relationship with Dracula changed her forever?

Find more discussion questions, visit www.harpercollins.com/readers

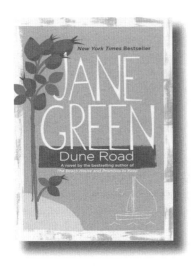

DUNE ROAD

Author: *Jane Green*

Publisher: Plume/Hudson St. Press, 2010

Website: www.us.penguingroup.com
www.janegreen.com

Available in: Trade Paperback
352 pages, $15.00, ISBN 978-0452296251

Also Available as: eBook and Audiobook

Subjects: Personal Discovery/
Relationships/Identity (Fiction)

"Green's newest has all the right elements for a sun-baked afternoon of reading: sandy locales, hints of sex and scandal, and lots of strong female characters." —**Publishers Weekly**

"Good as light vacation listening or for those anticipating a long car ride." —**Library Journal**

Summary: Kit Hargrove is trying to reinvent herself. Following her divorce, she is shedding the skin of her former life as the wife of a Wall Street high-roller and embracing both a new home and a new job as assistant to world famous novelist Robert McClore, all the while remaining close to her children and friends in the affluent Connecticut town of Highfield. Her transition seems to be going well until a series of events dramatically reminds her that nothing is ever quite as it seems. Kit's life is turned upside down when a long-lost sister she didn't know she had has an affair with her ex-husband. Secrets and lies force this once tight group of friends to question not only who they can believe, but who they can trust.

About the Author: **Jane Green** was born and brought up in London. Jane now lives in Connecticut, but flies home to London as often as four children and lots of animals allow. Jane's hugely successful books include; *Straight Talking, Jemima J., Mr Maybe, Bookends, Babyville, Spellbound, The Other Woman, Life Swap* and *Second Chance*.

CONVERSATION STARTERS

1. *Dune Road* offers a wide range of characters at different crucial moments in their lives. With which characters do you most identify? Which characters do you find most provocative?

2. What significance does the idea of feminine identity have in this book? In what ways does the book stray from female archetypes we see in other literature and media? In what ways does it agree with them?

3. The community of Highfield seems as much a character as any of the protagonists in the book. What role does social status play in *Dune Road*? How much pressure does it put on each character, if at all, and how does it drive their actions?

4. Annabel says, during a discussion with Kit, that "we are either born addicts, or not." Do you agree with this sentiment? What significance does fate have in the lives of *Dune Road*'s characters?

5. Kit and Edie have a conversation regarding the nature of marriage in which Kit bemoans the imperfections of her marriage to Adam while Edie argues that "a lot of the time that's all marriage is." With whom do you agree? Do you consider, as Kit often worries throughout the book, her reconciliation with Adam as a "step backward?"

6. Charlie and Keith suffer great loss at the hands of the economic recession. How do you feel about Charlie's anger toward Keith? Do you see Keith as a victim or as the guilty party? How important is it to you to share financial responsibility in a relationship?

7. What are the moral implications of Adam and Annabel's affair? Do you feel they were in the right to pursue each other or did they cross the line?

8. One of the most surprising things about Tracy's reconnection with Jed is that she sought him out on the Internet, despite a history of abuse. What does this say about the complex relationship between the abused and the abuser? What's your opinion of Tracy's actions throughout the book and how much control do you believe she had over her choices? Were they choices at all?

9. How have these characters changed during the course of the book? What surprised you about the ending? What future do you see for each of the characters?

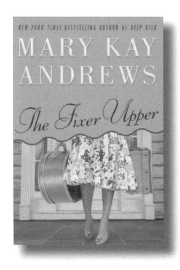

THE FIXER UPPER

AUTHOR: *Mary Kay Andrews*

PUBLISHER: Harper Paperbacks, 2010

WEBSITE: www.marykayandrews.com
www.harpercollins.com

AVAILABLE IN: Trade Paperback
448 pages, $14.99, ISBN 978-0060837396

ALSO AVAILABLE AS: eBook and Audiobook

SUBJECTS: Family/Personal Discovery/
Humor (Fiction)

"Entirely satisfying, an expert balance of warmth and compassion, terrific supporting characters, a little steamy sex, and just enough suspense to keep you from guessing how it will all go down."
—Atlanta Journal-Constitution

"This authentic tale of cleaning up life's messes and self-discovery is bright, engaging and thoughtful, enlivened by Andrews's quirky characters and lovely backwoods setting." —Publishers Weekly

SUMMARY: After her boss is caught in a political scandal, fledgling Washington lobbyist Dempsey Jo Killebrew is left broke, unemployed, and homeless. Out of options, she reluctantly accepts her father's offer to help turn Birdsong—the fading Victorian mansion he recently inherited in Guthrie, Georgia—into a real estate cash cow. But Birdsong turns out to be a moldering Pepto-Bismol-pink dump with duct-taped windows, a driveway full of junk, and a grumpy distant relation who's claiming squatter's rights. Stuck in a tiny town where everyone seems to know her business, Dempsey grits her teeth and rolls up her sleeves, and begins her journey back to the last place she ever expected: home.

ABOUT THE AUTHOR: **Mary Kay Andrews** is a *New York Times* bestselling author and a native of St. Petersburg, Florida. She wrote 10 critically acclaimed mysteries, including the *Callahan Garrity* mystery series, under her real name, **Kathy Hogan Trocheck**. Her new alias is a combination of her children's names. Married to her high school sweetheart, she mostly lives in Atlanta, although sometimes also on Tybee Island, Georgia.

CONVERSATION STARTERS

1. Dempsey is one tough cookie! Strong and independent, she weathers a major life upheaval without much hysteria and lets on to relatively few people what she is going through. What attitudes does she adopt and behaviors does she engage in to help her get through? How would your coping mechanisms compare to Dempsey's were you to find yourself in a similar situation?

2. Consider the level of support that Dempsey gets from her parents and friends. How do you think your family and friends would react if you were in a professional and legal predicament like Dempsey's? When support was offered, how did Dempsey respond?

3. When Dempsey's father sets her up at Birdsong, do you think his motives are entirely selfless? In what ways—financially, emotionally, otherwise—does it benefit him to have Dempsey go to Guthrie? Discuss his motivations. How does the dynamic of their father/daughter relationship compare with your own or with those of your loved ones? What is a "daddy's girl?" How can a daddy's girl grow up to be her own woman?

4. Bobby Livesey plays a huge role in the transformation of Birdsong. In what ways is Bobby also pivotal in Dempsey's personal transformation?

5. What is your take on Ella Kate's relationship with Dempsey's grandmother? How might their relationship be received differently today?

6. What do you think Dempsey saw in Jimmy Maynard initially that allowed her to be open to his flirtations? Why are smart women attracted to bad boys? What is the difference between a bad boy and a truly evil man?

7. What events in particular caused you to sympathize with Ella Kate? How does Jimmy Maynard redeem himself in your eyes over the course of the novel? How do Dempsey's relationship with and opinions of Lynda evolve over the course of her visit? How did yours?

8. Have you ever been screwed over by an employer or superior? If so, did it come as a shock and how did you react? Now that you've seen how Dempsey took care of her tormentor, how would you get the revenge of your dreams?

9. How do you imagine Dempsey's future life in Guthrie to be? Will she be content? What aspects of living there will pose the biggest challenge for her? Bring the most pleasure? How do you imagine her working relationship with Carter Berryhill to be different from hers with Alex Hodder?

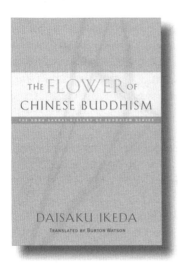

THE FLOWER OF CHINESE BUDDHISM

AUTHOR: *Daisaku Ikeda*
Burton Watson, Translator

PUBLISHER: Middleway Press, 2009

WEBSITE: www.middlewaypress.com
www.ikedabooks.org

AVAILABLE IN: Trade Paperback
176 pages, $14.95, ISBN 978-0977924547

SUBJECTS: Faith/History/Biography
(Nonfiction)

SUMMARY: *The Flower of Chinese Buddhism* illuminates the development and role of Buddhism in Chinese society, with the introduction of Buddhism into China by traders and monks traveling along the Silk Route. The author examines the career and achievements of Kumarajiva, famed for his philosophical treaties and translations that form the core of much Buddhist literature. Special emphasis is given to faith in the Lotus Sutra, affording the uninitiated reader a useful and accessible introduction to the school of Buddhism that was to become influential in Japan and the inspiration for the teachings of the 13th-century Buddhist reformer Nichiren.

ABOUT THE AUTHOR: **Daisaku Ikeda** is the author and coauthor of more than 60 books on a wide range of topics, including the history of Buddhism, Buddhist philosophy, dialogues with world leaders, poetry, novels and children's stories. He is the founding president and leader of the Soka Gakkai International, one of the largest lay Buddhist organizations in the world today. He is the recipient of the United Nations Peace Award, the Rosa Parks Humanitarian Award and the International Tolerance Award of the Simon Wiesenthal Center.

ABOUT THE TRANSLATOR: **Burton Watson** is a translator of Chinese and Japanese literature. His Translations include *Chuang Tzu: Basic Writings, The Lotus Sutra*, and *The Vimalakirti Sutra*, among others. He received the PEN Translation Prize in 1981.

CONVERSATION STARTERS

1. The author, Daisaku Ikeda, maintains that many aspects of the Buddhist religion facilitated its spread to different civilizations. Discuss what makes Buddhism uniquely acceptable throughout the world.

2. What were the obstacles to the spread of Buddhism in China? How were these overcome?

3. Kumarajiva is held to be the most famous translator of the Buddhist scriptures. What were his particular strengths, and why was he more successful than those who preceded him?

4. In early China, Buddhism was split between the northern and southern schools. How did this happen? Was this schism resolved?

5. In the beginning, the Buddhist faith was carried to China by people traveling from west to east along the Silk Road. This book relates the stories of those Chinese thinkers who made the opposite journey from China to India. What was their contribution to the spread of Buddhism in China?

6. The monk, Huisi, and his more famous disciple, Zhiyi (also known as The Great Teacher Tiantai), spent their lives in the study of the basic principles of the Lotus Sutra which constitute the core of Mahayana teaching. Discuss the importance of their writings.

7. In writing about the monk Xuanzang the author claims ". . . the teachings that Xuanzang espoused represent a doctrinal regression in the overall development of Buddhism in China." What leads the author to this conclusion?

8. Zhanran, one of the great foundational figures of Chinese Buddhism, lived during the Tang dynasty, a glorious era in Chinese culture. He became known as the restorer of the Tiantai school. What was the influence of his writings on the further spread of Buddhism across the Orient?

9. The author recounts the history of the persecution of Buddhism in Central Asia and China remarking that government oppression that forces people to abandon their faith sometimes awakens believers to value their faith more. Do you think that this is true? Can you see examples of this in today's world?

10. Buddhism evolved into a distinctive Chinese religion, influenced by older religions, which then spread to Korea and Japan. Has Chinese Buddhism influenced Buddhism in other parts of the world?

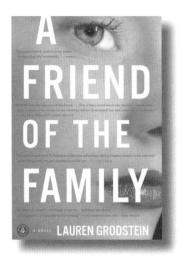

A FRIEND OF THE FAMILY

AUTHOR: *Lauren Grodstein*

PUBLISHER: Algonquin Books,
November 2010

WEBSITE: www.algonquin.com
www.laurengrodstein.com

AVAILABLE IN: Trade Paperback
320 pages, $13.95, ISBN 978-1616200176

ALSO AVAILABLE AS: eBook and Audiobook

SUBJECTS: Family/Personal Challenges/
Relationships (Fiction)

"Beautifully captures the ever striving angst of parents who will take any step to ensure their children's lives are easier or better." —**USA Today**

"Unfolds with suspense worthy of Hitchcock. . . . [Grodstein] is a terrific storyteller." —**The New York Times Book Review**

SUMMARY: Pete Dizinoff, a skilled and successful New Jersey internist, has a loving and devoted wife, a network of close friends, an impressive house, and, most of all, a son, Alec, now nineteen, on whom he has pinned all his hopes. But Pete hadn't expected his best friend's troubled daughter to set her sights on his boy. When Alec falls under her spell, Pete sets out to derail the romance, never foreseeing the devastating consequences.

In a riveting story of suburban tragedy, Lauren Grodstein charts a father's fall from grace as he struggles to save his family, his reputation, and himself.

ABOUT THE AUTHOR: **Lauren Grodstein** is the author of the collection *The Best of Animals* and a novel, *Reproduction is the Flaw of Love. A Friend of the Family* was a *Washington Post* Best Book, a *New York Times* Editors' Pick, and an Amazon Best Book of the Month. Her work has been translated into German, Italian, and French. She teaches creative writing at Rutgers University.

CONVERSATION STARTERS

1. Discuss whether you think Pete Dizinoff is a reliable narrator—that is, whether you believe his account of the events in the story from beginning to end. Much of the novel is composed of Pete's memories, but how do we know whether we can trust what he says? Are there such things as reliable memories?

2. How do you think Elaine's struggle with breast cancer affects her perspective on Alec's future? Do you think her illness shapes her attitude?

3. Discuss Pete's responsibility in the death of Roseanne Craig.

4. Pete is mystified at Laura's pregnancy, since when he was in high school, "nobody had sex with the Laura Sterns" (page 29). How is teenage sexuality presented in this novel? Is it a refuge? A crime? A normal part of adolescence?

5. As a culture, we seem to expect life-altering friendships between women, not men. How does this book explore male friendship? How does this friendship differ from the friendships between the women in this book?

6. What is the relationship between Joe and his father like in this book? What is the relationship between Joe and his older son, Neal, like? How does Pete assess these relationships when considering his own with his father and his son?

7. How are the families in this novel twinned? In what respect is Joe's parenting of Laura a mirror of Pete's parenting of Alec?

8. There are five deaths mentioned in this book: those of Joe's father, Pete's father, Laura Stern's baby, Roseanne Craig, and Louis Sherman, the patient who died of septicemia. All physicians encounter death, of course, but how do these particular deaths shape Pete as a person? As a doctor?

9. Of all the relationships in this novel, the most important might be Pete's relationship with the reader. What does Pete want from his reader? What does Pete need his reader to believe, and why?

10. During her confrontation with Pete at her apartment, Laura Stern refuses to change out of her flimsy pajamas. Why won't she change her clothing? Why does Pete smoke her cigarettes?

11. How important is Pete's Jewish heritage to the story of this novel? How important are his beginnings in Yonkers?

12. Why do you think Elaine stays with Pete at the end of the book?

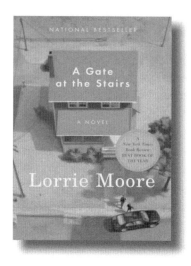

A GATE AT THE STAIRS

AUTHOR: *Lorrie Moore*

PUBLISHER: Vintage Books, 2010

WEBSITE: www.ReadingGroupCenter.com

AVAILABLE IN: Trade Paperback
336 pages, $15.00, ISBN 978-0375708466

ALSO AVAILABLE AS: eBook

SUBJECTS: Family/Social Issues/
American History (Fiction)

"Profound. . . . Get ready to expand your sense of what Moore—and a novel—can do." —The Washington Post Book World

*"Her most powerful book yet. . . . An indelible portrait of a young woman coming of age in the Midwest." —***Michiko Kakutani, *The New York Times*

SUMMARY: Tassie Keltjin has come from a small farming town to attend college in Troy, "the Athens of the Midwest." She's swept into a thrilling world of books and films and riveting lectures, high-flying discussions about Bach, Balkanization, and bacterial warfare, and the witty repartee of her fellow students. At the end of the semester, Tassie takes a job as a part-time nanny for the newly adopted child of Sarah Brink, the owner of a trendy downtown restaurant, and her husband, Edward Thornwood, a scientist pursuing independent research. Tassie is enchanted by the little girl. Her feelings about Sarah and Edward are less easily defined, and as she becomes an integral part of their family, the mysteries of their lives and their relationship only deepen. She finds little to anchor her: a boyfriend turns out to be quite different from what he seems; vacations in her hometown are like visits to an alien country; and her loving, eccentric family no longer provides the certainties and continuity that shaped her childhood.

ABOUT THE AUTHOR: **Lorrie Moore** is the author of the story collections *Birds of America, Like Life*, and *Self-Help* and the novels *Who Will Run the Frog Hospital?* and *Anagrams*. She has been the recipient of fellowships from the National Endowment for the Arts, the Guggenheim Foundation, the Lannan Foundation, and the Rockefeller Foundation.

CONVERSATION STARTERS

1. In addition to her sense of humor and intelligence, what are Tassie's strengths as a narrator? How does what she describes as "an unseemly collection of jostling former selves" (p. 63) affect the narrative and contribute to the appeal of her tale?

2. How does the initial meeting between Tassie and Sarah (pp. 10–24) create a real, if hesitant, connection between them? What aspects of their personalities come out in their conversation? To what extent are their impressions of each other influenced by their personal needs, both practical and psychological?

3. Are Sarah's ill-chosen comments at the meetings with Amber (p. 32) and Bonnie (pp. 89–90, p. 93) the result of the natural awkwardness between a birth mother and a potential adoptive mother or do they reveal deeper insecurities in Sarah? Does the adoption process inevitably involve a certain amount of willful deception, unenforceable promises (p. 87), and a "ceremony of approval . . . [that is] as with all charades. . . . wanly ebullient, necessary, and thin" (p. 95)?

4. Does *A Gate at the Stairs* accurately reflect the persistence of racism in America? What do the comments and encounters sprinkled throughout in the novel (pp. 80, 112, 151, 167, 229) show about the various forms racism takes in our society?

5. The title of the book comes from a ballad Tassie writes with her roommate (p. 219–20). What does music-playing the bass and singing to Mary-Emma-represent to Tassie? How does it connect her to her own family and to Mary-Emma?

6. Does the Midwestern setting of the novel offer a distinctive perspective on September 11, 2001, and the mood of the country? How were the events experienced in other parts of America-for example, in the cities directly affected by the terrorist attacks?

7. Lorrie Moore has been widely praised for her affecting depictions of human vulnerability and her dark humor. How does Moore integrate clever one-liners, puns, and wordplay into the serious themes she is exploring? What role does humor play in exposing the thoughts, feelings, and fears the characters are unwilling or unable to express? Does it heighten the emotional force of the novel or diminish it?

8. "I had also learned that in literature-perhaps as in life-one had to speak not of what the author intended but of what a story intended for itself" (p. 263–64]. How does this quotation apply to your reading of *A Gate at the Stairs*?

THE GIRL WHO FELL FROM THE SKY

Author: *Heidi W. Durrow*

Publisher: Algonquin Books, January 2011

Website: www.algonquin.com
www.heidiwdurrow.com

Available in: Trade Paperback
272 pages, $13.95, ISBN 978-1616200152

Also Available as: eBook and Audiobook

Subjects: Social Issues/Women's Lives/
Identity (Fiction)

"An auspicious debut. . . . [Durrow] has crafted a modern story about identity and survival." —**Washington Post**

"[An] affecting, exquisite debut novel . . . Durrow's powerful novel is poised to find a place among classic stories of the American experience."
—**Miami Herald**

Summary: Rachel, the daughter of a Danish mother and a black G.I., becomes the sole survivor of a family tragedy after a fateful morning on their Chicago rooftop.

Forced to move to a new city, with her strict African American grandmother as her guardian, Rachel is thrust for the first time into a mostly black community, where her light brown skin, blue eyes, and beauty bring a constant stream of attention her way. It's there, as she grows up and tries to swallow her grief, that she comes to understand how the mystery and tragedy of her mother might be connected to her own uncertain identity.

About the Author: A graduate of Stanford University, Columbia University's Graduate School of Journalism, and Yale Law School, Heidi W. Durrow has received numerous grants for her writing. Her debut novel, *The Girl Who Fell from the Sky*, is the winner of the 2009 Bellwether Prize for fiction that addresses issues of social injustice, awarded by Barbara Kingsolver.

CONVERSATION STARTERS

1. *The Girl Who Fell from the Sky* is set in the 1980s. How does its chronological setting affect its plot and themes? Do you think the novel's events might play out any differently if it were set in contemporary times?

2. Rachel's grandma notes proudly that she was the first African American woman to buy a house in her Portland, Oregon, neighborhood. Does the geographic setting reflect the novel's themes in any way? How might the story, or Grandma's character, or Rachel's coming-of-age, be different had the story been set in the Deep South?

3. The image of Rachel's family falling from the sky is horrific, especially when it's described from Jamie's point of view. How does the reader come to understand what happened in that scene? How did you feel on making that discovery?

4. Why does Jamie decide to change his name to Brick? What is the significance in his renaming himself? Does he get what he claims he wanted, "a new history to his name" (page 42)?

5. When does Rachel first become aware of her racial difference? What does it mean for her identity when she starts to see herself as the "new girl" (page 10)? How does her understanding of her identity continue to evolve during the novel?

5. The word *nigger* is used many times in the novel. What kind of personal reaction did you have to reading this word repeatedly? Do you think the author uses the word effectively in this context? What does Nella's observation that "if she is just a word then she doesn't have me" (page 243) mean?

7. Issues of sex, violence, and romantic love are wrapped up with each other throughout the novel. In what ways do ideas about sex and love become twisted? Does the book depict any positive romantic and/or sexual relationships?

8. What is Brick's motivation for following Rachel? Does knowing the story that he learns from Rachel's father help you understand Nella's motivations more fully?

9. What insights into Nella's character and motivations do you gain from reading her journal entries? What do you think of Laronne's belief that Nella "was journeying to where her love was enough, and it could fill the sky" (page 156)?

10. Imagery of flying and falling runs throughout the novel. Are these two concepts always opposites? At the end, is Rachel more inspired to fall or to fly?

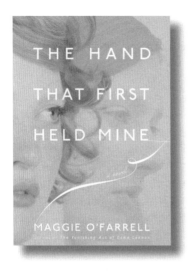

THE HAND THAT FIRST HELD MINE

AUTHOR: *Maggie O'Farrell*

PUBLISHER: Houghton Mifflin Harcourt, 2010

WEBSITE: www.houghtonmifflinbooks.com
www.maggieofarrell.com

AVAILABLE IN: Hardcover
352 pages, $25.00, ISBN 978-0547330792

ALSO AVAILABLE AS: eBook

SUBJECTS: History/Women's Lives/
Relationships (Fiction)

"An exquisitely sensual tale of love, motherhood, and other forms of madness, The Hand That First Held Mine *will unsettle, move, and haunt you."* —**Emma Donoghue, author of *Room* and *Slammerkin***

"Maggie O'Farrell's cinematically vivid novel is moody and powerful and plotted at a breakneck pace. This book, like life, will disarm you with its unannounced twists and tragedies and moments of unexpected beauty. She delivers to readers that rarest of experiences—total emotional investment. Hers is a brilliant feat of prose marksmanship—also, it made me cry on the subway." —**Heidi Julavits, author of *The Effect of Living Backwards* and *The Uses of Enchantment***

SUMMARY: *The Hand That First Held Mine* is a spellbinding novel of two women connected across fifty years by art, love, betrayals, secrets, and motherhood. Like her acclaimed *The Vanishing Act of Esme Lennox*, it is a "breathtaking, heart-breaking creation." And it is a gorgeous inquiry into the ways we make and unmake our lives, who we know ourselves to be, and how even our most accidental legacies connect us.

ABOUT THE AUTHOR: **Maggie O'Farrell** is the author of four previous novels, including the acclaimed *The Vanishing Act of Esme Lennox*, which was a B&N Recommends Pick, and *After You'd Gone*. Born in Northern Ireland in 1972, O'Farrell grew up in Wales and Scotland. She has two children.

CONVERSATION STARTERS

1. Discuss the "firsts" referred to in the title. How were Lexie's beliefs about love and life transformed by Innes? Is there a "first" in your past who changed the course of your life?

2. How did your impressions of Elina and Ted change throughout the novel? What assumptions did you make after reading their opening scene?

3. Describe the different faces of love presented in *The Hand That First Held Mine*. Which lovers experienced equal affection? Which relationship appealed to you the most?

4. Did you believe Innes's claim that Gloria had been unfaithful to him, and that Margot was not his biological daughter?

5. Discuss the paintings that became Lexie's final connection to Innes. What value did they have to Lexie, and to Innes? What value did Margot place on them? What motivated collectors to assign a high financial value to them?

6. How do Elina and Ted each emerge from their periods of instability? To what degree is deception (including self-deception) at the root of their anguish?

7. Discuss the various types of mothering portrayed in the novel. Do Gloria, Margot, Lexie, and Elina share any common ground in their expectations of motherhood? As an artist, did Elina approach motherhood with a different perspective?

8. When Lexie struggles in the waters off the Dorset coast, she can think only of Theo and imagines the milestones he will experience. How did motherhood change her? How did she blend motherhood with her career? What made her a great, if unconventional, mother?

9. What portraits of the world do Lexie and Elina create in their careers? What talents do artists and art critics share?

10. How do the men in Lexie's life compare to each other? What enabled her to find peace and trust with Robert?

11. Who has the most power in the relationships depicted in *The Hand That First Held Mine*? Was Innes vulnerable to Lexie, despite her inexperience and youth? What gave Margot power over Felix?

12. How does Elina's Finnish identity enhance her relationship with Ted? Does it help her to be seen as an outsider?

13. How are fate and revelation woven throughout each of Maggie O'Farrell's novels, including her best-selling debut, *After You'd Gone*? What is unique about her portrayal of love in *The Hand That First Held Mine*?

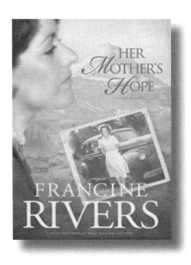

HER MOTHER'S HOPE
Marta's Legacy

AUTHOR: *Francine Rivers*

PUBLISHER: Tyndale House Publishers, 2010

WEBSITE: www.tyndale.com
www.francinerivers.com

AVAILABLE IN: Hardcover
512 pages, $24.99, ISBN 978-1414318639

ALSO AVAILABLE AS: eBook

SUBJECTS: Family/Faith/Personal Discovery (Fiction)

"This well-told tale will have readers eagerly awaiting the story's resolution." —**Publishers Weekly**

SUMMARY: Near the turn of the 20th century, fiery Marta leaves Switzerland determined to find life on her own terms. Her journey takes her through Europe and finally lands her with children and husband in tow in the central valley of California. Marta's experiences convince her that only the strong survive. Hildie, Marta's oldest daughter, has a heart to serve others, and her calling as a nurse gives her independence, if not the respect of her mother.

Amid the drama of WWII, Hildie marries and begins a family of her own. She wants her daughter never to doubt her love—but the challenges of life conspire against her vow. Each woman is forced to confront her faulty but well-meaning desire to help her daughter find her God-given place in the world.

ABOUT THE AUTHOR: **Francine Rivers**, a *New York Times* bestselling author, began her literary career at the University of Nevada, Reno, where she graduated with a Bachelor of Arts degree in English and Journalism. From 1976 to 1985, she had a successful writing career in the general market and her books were awarded or nominated for numerous awards and prizes. Although raised in a religious home, Francine did not truly encounter Christ until later in life, when she was already a wife, mother of three, and an established romance novelist.

CONVERSATION STARTERS

1. Marta certainly had a difficult childhood. What factors do you think shaped her the most, for better or worse? How do you see those influences shape the woman she becomes?

2. How does Marta's father shape her early beliefs about God and His expectations of her? Contrast that with the way her mama talks about God. What seems to make the biggest impression on the way Marta views God? Do you see that change throughout the story? If so, what causes that change?

3. Marta has a hard time trusting Niclas because of the way her father treated her mother. How do you think that made Niclas feel? How was he able to love Marta despite her sometimes prickly nature? In what ways—good or bad—has your family of origin affected your marriage or close friendships?

4. Do you feel like it was right for Niclas to ask Marta to sell the boarding house and move to Manitoba with him? Why was it so difficult for her? What did the boardinghouse represent for her? If you were Marta, what would you have done in that situation?

5. Do you think Marta hijacked Niclas's role as head of their household? In what ways was Niclas both passive and aggressive? Did Marta view herself as a "helpmate" to Niclas, and do you think he saw her in that way?

6. Why do you think that Marta was so averse to Hildemara's decision to attend nursing school? Does she ever change her mind about Hildemara's chosen profession?

7. Tuberculosis is much rarer today than it was in Marta's and Hildemara's lifetimes. Yet life-threatening and chronic illnesses have never been more prevalent. How has your family been impacted by serious illness? Discuss the strain illness can place on family dynamics, regardless of the "relational health" a family may have at the outset.

8. At the end of this book Marta is determined, with God's help, to make a fresh start with Hildemara. Do you think she will succeed? Why or why not? How do you think Hildemara will respond? Is there hope for this relationship?

9. If you could change one thing about the way you were parented, what would it be? And if you have children, is there anything you would change about the way you've parented them thus far?

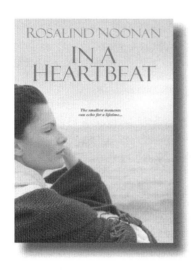

IN A HEARTBEAT

Author: *Rosalind Noonan*

Publisher: Kensington Trade Paperback, 2010

Website: www.kensingtonbooks.com
www.rosalindnoonan.com

Available in: Trade Paperback
512 pages, $15.00, ISBN 978-0758241672

Also Available as: eBook

Subjects: Family/Personal Challenges/ Intrigue (Fiction)

Praise for previous novel, *One September Morning*
"Noonan delivers a fast-paced, character-driven tale with a touch of mystery."—Publishers Weekly

Summary: Kate McGann is wrenched from sleep by the 3 a.m. phone call every parent dreads. Her nineteen-year-old son, Ben, is lying unconscious in a Syracuse hospital after being attacked in his sleep by an unknown assailant with a baseball bat.

While Kate waits, frantically wishing for Ben to wake up and take back his life, she tries to uncover who could have done something so brutal. Ben's talent as a baseball player on his college team made some teammates jealous, but could any of them have hated him enough to do this? The crisis brings all of Ben's relationships into sharp focus—and also leads Kate to unsettling revelations about her marriage. And with each discovery, Kate learns what happens when a single unforeseen event changes everything, and the future you've taken for granted is snatched away in a heartbeat.

About the Author: **Rosalind Noonan** grew up in suburban Maryland and enjoyed being part of a large family. She attended Wagner College in Staten Island. After graduation she worked in New York City as an editor and copywriter for various book publishers. She has studied writing for screen and theater at The New School. She currently lives in the Pacific Northwest with her husband and their two children.

CONVERSATION STARTERS

1. The call Kate McGann receives at the beginning of the book sets inevitable changes in motion. Have you ever received a life-changing phone call like Kate's? Or was there a defining moment in your life that set off major changes?

2. *In a Heartbeat* is written from multiple viewpoints. Did you find it jarring to transition from one character's point of view to another's, or did you enjoy jumping into a different person's thoughts?

3. Which character(s) did you most enjoy spending time with? Do you find that you prefer reading about people you relate to, or characters who expose you to a different culture or worldview?

4. With much advancement in medicine, health advocacy has become more important than ever. Do you think Kate made the right choices as her son's advocate? If you were in her place, what might you have done differently?

5. Although Emma is quick to remove herself from her relationship with Ben, what do you think she learns from this experience?

6. Revenge is a recurring theme throughout *In a Heartbeat*. Explain how it applies to the players on the Lakers team. How does it affect Kate? Would you say revenge is Dylan's primary stimulus, or were his actions the result of complex motivations?

7. When Marnie searches her conscience for someone who might have a vendetta against her, she comes up with an incident from her childhood when she caused emotional harm to someone. Considering her age at the time, do you think her mother should have pursued it further? Do you think her father's response was appropriate?

8. Both Kate and Eli have been keeping secrets through the course of their relationship. If they were honest in the beginning of their relationship, do you think things would have turned out differently?

9. At the end of the book, when Kate and Eli talk about fathering Ben, there is a new dimension to their discussion. How has Eli's approach to parenting been changed by the events of the story?

10. How do Kate's feelings toward Eli evolve through the course of the novel?

11. If you were casting *In a Heartbeat* for a film, whom would you choose to play Kate and Cody? Marnie and Ben?

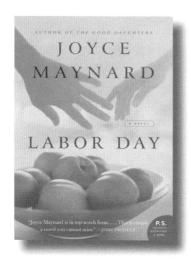

LABOR DAY

Author: *Joyce Maynard*

Publisher: Harper Perennial, 2010

Website: www.harperperennial.com
www.joycemaynard.com

Available in: Trade Paperback
272 pages, $13.99, ISBN 978-0061843419

Also Available as: eBook and Audiobook

Subjects: Coming of Age/Identity/
Personal Discovery (Fiction)

"Joyce Maynard is in top-notch form with Labor Day. *From the perfect pitch of a teenaged boy narrator to the eloquent message of how loneliness can bind people together, this is simply a novel you cannot miss."*
—**Jodi Picoult,** *New York Times* **bestselling author of** *My Sister's Keeper* **and** *Handle With Care*

Summary: With the end of summer closing in and a steamy Labor Day weekend looming in the town of Holton Mills, New Hampshire, thirteen-year-old Henry—lonely, friendless, not too good at sports—spends most of his time watching television, reading, and daydreaming about the soft skin and budding bodies of his female classmates. But all that changes on the Thursday before Labor Day, when a mysterious bleeding man named Frank approaches Henry and asks for a hand. Over the next five days, Henry will learn some of life's most valuable lessons and the knowledge that real love is worth waiting for.

Joyce Maynard weaves a beautiful, poignant tale of love, sex, adolescence, and devastating treachery as seen through the eyes of a young teenage boy—and the man he later becomes—looking back at an unexpected encounter that begins one single long, hot, life-altering weekend.

About the Author: **Joyce Maynard** has been a reporter for the *New York Times*, a magazine journalist, radio commentator, and syndicated columnist, as well as the author of five novels. Her bestselling memoir *At Home in the World* has been translated into nine languages.

CONVERSATION STARTERS

1. As reported by Henry, his mother Adele displays a number of behaviors that could be interpreted as crazy. How do you explain her son's steadiness and competence? Do you consider Adele to be a bad mother?

2. When you were first introduced to the character of Frank (p. 5), what was your feeling about him? As you learned more about Frank over the course of the story, did your impression of him change? If so, what details and actions can you identify that caused you to alter your opinion of him?

3. Were you surprised that Adele was willing to bring Frank to her home? Why do you think she did?

4. Henry's father and his wife, Marjorie, live a much more steady and "normal" life than the one Henry shares with Adele. Why do you think Henry remains so loyal to his mother, concealing aspects of her behavior that would no doubt alarm his father?

5. What was your first impression of the character of Eleanor? Did this impression change as you got to know her better? Why do you think Eleanor behaves as she does?

6. How does Eleanor go about instilling fear and doubts about Frank in Henry? Why do you think she does this? What is she hoping to accomplish?

7. In Chapter 18 Henry comments that seeing his mother happy with Frank "took me off the hook." At the same time, he appears to be threatened by the possibility that the intimacy she has discovered with Frank will cause her to abandon him. How does Henry go about reconciling these two conflicting responses to the love affair he witnesses, and how much of what takes place occurs as a result of this conflict?

8. How do you think the events of that Labor Day weekend changed Henry? How might his life have gone if Frank had not shown up?

9. Why do you think Adele relinquishes custody of Henry? Why does he decide to return to her?

10. Were you surprised by what Henry says and does when he encounters Eleanor again, a year later, walking her dog?

11. Frank's experience with Adele and Henry cost him eighteen years of his life, and yet he expresses gratitude for having met them. How can this be? Do you believe the kind of love that existed between Adele and Frank can truly exist?

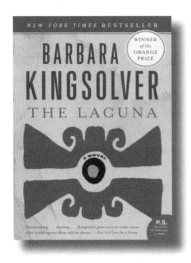

THE LACUNA

AUTHOR: *Barbara Kingsolver*

PUBLISHER: Harper Perennial, 2010

WEBSITE: www.harperperennial.com
www.kingsolver.com

AVAILABLE IN: Trade Paperback
544 pages, $16.99, ISBN 978-0060852580

ALSO AVAILABLE AS: eBook and Audiobook

SUBJECTS: History/Social Issues/Art
(Fiction)

"Rich . . . impassioned . . . engrossing. . . . Politics and art dominate the novel, and their overt, unapologetic connection is refreshing." —**Chicago Tribune**

"Compelling. . . . Kingsolver's descriptions of life in Mexico City burst with sensory detail—thick sweet breads, vividly painted walls, the lovely white feet of an unattainable love." —**The New Yorker**

SUMMARY: In this powerfully imagined, provocative novel, Barbara Kingsolver takes us on an epic journey from the Mexico of artists Diego Rivera and Frida Kahlo to the America of Pearl Harbor, FDR, and J. Edgar Hoover. *The Lacuna* is the poignant story of a man pulled between two nations as well as an unforgettable portrait of the artist—and of art itself.

ABOUT THE AUTHOR: **Barbara Kingsolver** is the author of seven works of fiction, including the novels *The Lacuna, The Poisonwood Bible, Animal Dreams, and The Bean Trees*, as well as books of poetry, essays, and creative nonfiction. Her most recent work of nonfiction is the enormously influential bestseller *Animal, Vegetable, Miracle: A Year of Food Life*. Kingsolver's work has been translated into more than twenty languages and has earned literary awards and a devoted readership at home and abroad. In 2000, she was awarded the National Humanities Medal, our country's highest honor for service through the arts. She lives with her family on a farm in southern Appalachia.

CONVERSATION STARTERS

1. The word "lacuna" means many things: a missing piece of a manuscript, a gap in history or knowledge, a tunnel or passage leading from one place to another. What are some of the lacunae in this novel?

2. Several characters repeat the phrase: "The most important part of a story is the piece of it you don't know." What does this mean to you, in terms of both public and private life? Are you likely to give this consideration more weight, since reading the novel?

3. Given the unusual presentation of the novel, as diary entries written by a person who does not want to be known, how did you come to know Harrison Shepherd? Which of his passions or dreads evoked a connection for you?

4. The opening paragraph of the novel promises: "In the beginning were the howlers," and suggests they will always be with us. As you read, did you find yourself thinking of modern occasions of media "howlers" purveying gossip, fear, and injurious misquotes? Why does this industry persist? Has an increasingly rapid news cycle changed its power?

5. Did any historical revelations in this novel surprise you? How has our national character changed from earlier times? How would we now respond, for example, to the universal rationing imposed during World War II? Or to the later events aimed at containing "un-American activities?" What elements shape these responses? What is the value, in your opinion, of the historical novel as a genre?

6. What places or sensory events in the novel appealed to you most? Are you a more visual, auditory, or olfactory sort of person? What sensory impressions stayed with you after you had finished the book?

7. The two important women in Harrison Shepherd's life, Violet Brown and Frida Kahlo, seem to be opposites at first glance. Do they also share similarities? What cemented the relationships, in each case? Do you find these women, in their similar or opposing ways, emblematic of women's modes of adapting to difficulty, or exerting power?

8. On page 424, Arthur Gold complains that patriotism is coming to be defined as intolerance of dissent, and that the consequences could be dangerous. What do you think of his diagnosis? How do you interpret his advice that anti-communism has nothing to do with communism?

9. Do you believe the novel ended with optimism, or sadness?

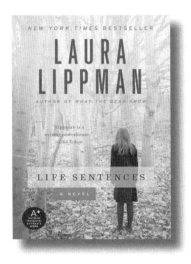

LIFE SENTENCES

AUTHOR: *Laura Lippman*

PUBLISHER: Avon A, 2010

WEBSITE: www.lauralippman.com
www.harpercollins.com

AVAILABLE IN: Trade Paperback
368 pages, $14.99, ISBN 978-0061944888

ALSO AVAILABLE AS: eBook and Audiobook

SUBJECTS: Mystery/Social Issues/
Women's Lives (Fiction)

"From its gripping opening pages . . . Life Sentences *may be the most absorbing, entertaining mystery published in the last year. Lippman does it all, from creating vivid, three-dimensional characters, to painting a beautifully detailed portrait of her hometown, Baltimore, to crafting a plot that drives readers along at a fast clip while simultaneously building suspense as one dramatic revelation leads to another."* —**Boston Globe**

SUMMARY: Author Cassandra Fallows believes she may have found the story that could become her next bestseller. When she was a girl growing up in a racially diverse middle-class neighborhood in Baltimore, a shy, quiet, unobtrusive child named Calliope Jenkins orbited Cassandra's circle of friends. Later Calliope would be accused of an unspeakable crime and would spend seven years in prison for refusing to speak about it. But by delving too deeply into Calliope's dark secrets, Cassandra may inadvertently unearth a few of her own—forcing her to reexamine the memories she holds most precious, as the stark light of truth illuminates a mother's pain, a father's betrayal . . . and what really transpired on a terrible day that devastated not only a family but an entire country.

ABOUT THE AUTHOR: **Laura Lippman** grew up in Baltimore and returned to her hometown in 1989 to work as a journalist. After writing seven books while still a full-time reporter, she left *The Baltimore Sun* to focus on fiction. She is the author of multiple *New York Times* bestsellers including *What the Dead Know* and *Life Sentences*.

CONVERSATION STARTERS

1. *Life Sentences* suggests that stories belong to whomever tells them. Is that fair, unfair? Under what circumstances, if any, does a story—a life—belong only to the person who lived it?

2. Is Cassandra a likable person, or at least an ethical one? Does it matter if she's likable?

3. Was Cassandra's memoir, *Her Father's Daughter*, "true"?

4. What do you think happened to Callie's son? Does she tell Cassandra the truth, or the truth as she needs to believe it? Is there a difference?

5. *Life Sentences* has many references to myths and folk tales—stories of the ancient Greeks, but also Br'er Rabbit. What myths do the characters need in order to go about their day-to-day lives? Does Tisha have a myth that sustains her? Gloria Bustamante?

6. Cassandra is white, most of her childhood friends were African-American (as was her stepmother), and Gloria Bustamante is Latina. But is race that central to the story of *Life Sentences*? In what ways?

7. Why does Lenore allow her husband's version of events to stand uncontested?

8. Is Cedric Fallows self-aware? Does he have any sense of the way he has affected his daughter?

9. What has Cassandra learned beyond the facts of her own life and Callie's life? Does she change over the course of this book? In what ways? Would the Cassandra we meet in that opening chapter make the same choices that Cassandra makes at the book's end?

10. What point is Tisha trying to make when she shows Cassandra a small inaccuracy in *Her Father's Daughter*?

11. On the last page of the novel, Callie passes a sign that Cassandra has also noticed: If you lived here, you would be home by now. Cassandra had wondered if the sign was a tautology, or at least mildly redundant. But Callie responds to the sign very differently. What does this tell us about Cassandra and Callie? Where is Callie—in her life—at the book's end? Has she found a home in the world? Has she at last made all the lies true?

Find more discussion questions, visit www.harpercollins.com/readers

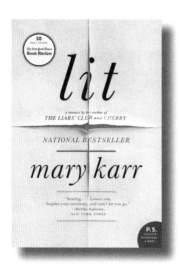

LIT
A Memoir

AUTHOR: *Mary Karr*

PUBLISHER: Harper Perennial, 2010

WEBSITE: www.harperperennial.com

AVAILABLE IN: Trade Paperback
432 pages, $14.99, ISBN 978-0060596996

ALSO AVAILABLE AS: eBook and Audiobook

SUBJECTS: Social Issues/Family/
Relationships (Memoir)

"Searing. . . . A book that lassos you, hogties your emotions and won't let you go. . . . Chronicles with searching intelligence, humor and grace the author's slow, sometimes exhilarating, sometimes painful discovery of her vocation and her voice as a poet and writer." —**Michiko Kakutani, New York Times**

"Karr tells the story with the same down-to-earth writing-some of it funny-that she brought to her first two memoirs. . . . Her willingness to show herself in this light and the humility with which she writes about recovery and faith are testaments to the honesty of both her writing and her life." —**Nancy Connors, *Cleveland Plain Dealer***

SUMMARY: *Lit* is about getting drunk and getting sober; becoming a mother by letting go of a mother; learning to write by learning to live. Written with Karr's relentless honesty, unflinching self-scrutiny, and irreverent, lacerating humor, it is a truly electrifying story of how to grow up—as only Mary Karr can tell it.

ABOUT THE AUTHOR: **Mary Karr** is a Guggenheim Fellow in poetry. She has won Pushcart Prizes for both verse and essays, and is the Peck Professor of Literature at Syracuse University. Her previous two memoirs, *The Liars' Club* and *Cherry*, were *New York Times* bestsellers.

CONVERSATION STARTERS

1. The first sentence of *Lit* is "Any way I tell this story is a lie." What does Mary mean by this? Is she a reliable storyteller? Is there a story in your family famous for its different versions? Is there a story you can't tell without "feeling" like it's partially untrue?

2. Mary refers to her mother as "a shadow stitched" to her feet and to herself and her mother as "dovetailing drunks" and as facing off "like a pair of mirrors". What does this say about Mary's relationship with her mother? Do all women feel this way about their moms? At what age is it most painful? At what age—if any—does it end?

3. Mary writes, "I sense the oppressive weight of my old self inside me pressing to run wild again. My old mother I'm trying to keep in." Have you ever found yourself wincing at how you resemble your mother?

4. How is Mary's trip to college with Mother the "hairpin", as she describes it, in her early life? This trip marks her introduction to real drinking, but it's also the point at which Mary would "start furnishing [Mother] with reading instead of the other way around." What does Mary mean by this, and what's the significance of this transition? Was there an "official" transition to adulthood in your life? Was it marked by college, marriage, parenthood, career success, or something else?

5. "Words shape our realities," Mary concludes when she registers the meaning of the Ernst Cassirer quote: "The same function which the image of God performs, the same tendency to permanent existence, may be ascribed to the uttered sound of language". How does this realization frame Mary's determination to become a poet? At what times do religion and poetry seem to do the same things for her?

6. Mary has "mysterious blanks" in her memory of fights with Warren. What are the glaring blanks in your own memory? Do you think these are genuine blanks of memories or memories that you have chosen to block out?

7. In what ways does Mary's son Dev save her? If she had lost custody of him in a divorce, would she still have gotten sober? How have your children made you better, at time, or ground you to a nub in others?

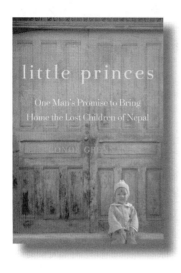

LITTLE PRINCES
One Man's Promise to Bring Home the Lost Children of Nepal

AUTHOR: *Conor Grennan*

PUBLISHER: William Morrow, January 2011

WEBSITE: www.harpercollins.com
www.conorgrennan.net

AVAILABLE IN: Hardcover
304 pages, $25.99, ISBN 978-0061930058

ALSO AVAILABLE AS: eBook and Audiobook

SUBJECTS: Inspiration/Social Issues/
Family (Memoir)

"Funny, touching, tragic . . . a remarkable tale of . . . one man's extraordinary quest to reunite lost children with their parents." —**Neil White, author of *In the Sanctuary of Outcasts***

"More than just another do-gooder's tale from the trenches, Conor's book is both an inspiring story of service and a page-turning adventure." —**Bryan Mealer, co-author of *The Boy Who Harnessed the Wind***

SUMMARY: In need of some fun and adventure, 30-year-old Conor Grennan traded in his day job for a year-long trip around the globe, a journey that began with a three-month stint volunteering at the Little Princes Orphanage in war-torn Nepal. But what began as a lark became a passionate commitment that would transform the young American and the lives of countless others.

Within minutes of his arrival, Grennan was surrounded by a horde of gleeful boys and girls showering him with warm welcomes. Yet as he soon learned, the children's cheery smiles belied years of pain and abuse, for many of the boys and girls at Little Princes were not orphans at all, but victims rescued from human traffickers. Moved by their plight, Grennan vowed that when his trip was over he would return to the children of Little Princes and eventually reunite them with their families—a promise he would risk his life to keep.

ABOUT THE AUTHOR: **Conor Grennan** serves as an active board member for Next Generation Nepal and is still involved in the daily activity of the organization. He lives in the New York City area with his wife and son.

CONVERSATION STARTERS

1. What most impressed you about the author and the children with whom he came into contact? Did any aspect of the story upset you? Did Conor's story inspire you?

2. In your opinion, what was it about these children that touched Conor so deeply? Were you moved by their plight? What about the increasing number of children growing up in poverty in America? Do you see these children in the same way, or do you see their situations differently?

3. How might American children help their counterparts in places like Nepal? Thinking about the Little Princes, do you think we as Americans spoil our children and ourselves—do we buy more than what can truly be appreciated?

4. When Conor returned to Nepal he met the mother of one of the Little Princes. How did this affect him personally? And how did it influence the course of events that followed?

5. How did volunteering at Little Princes prepare Conor for having a family of his own? What did these children teach him about himself and the world?

6. At the beginning of *Little Princes*, Conor did not see himself as a global humanitarian, yet his visit to Nepal changed everything. What is it about him—and others like him introduced in Little Princes—that sets him apart from those who don't volunteer or get involved?

7. How did Golkka, the man who trafficked many of these children, get away with his nefarious practices for so long? Human trafficking has become a worldwide problem, affecting millions. Why has it flourished and what steps might help stop it? How might you play a role? Would you consider doing so? Why or why not?

8. Do you empathize with the parents of the Little Princes children and others? Do you understand why they gave their children up? What might you do given similar circumstances?

9. What lessons did you take away from reading *Little Princes*?

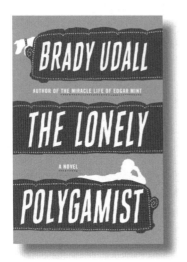

THE LONELY POLYGAMIST

Author: *Brady Udall*

Publisher: W.W. Norton & Company, 2010

Website: www.wwnorton.com
www.bradyudall.com

Available in: Hardcover
602 pages, $26.95, ISBN 978-0393062625

Also Available as: eBook

Subjects: Family/Personal Challenges/
Relationships (Fiction)

"A superb performance. . . . Udall's polished storytelling and sterling cast of perfectly realized and flawed characters make this a serious contender for Great American Novel status." —**Publishers Weekly (starred review)**

"A brilliantly crafted mini-epic that is at turns hilarious, terrifying, and heartbreaking. . . . Cinematic. . . . A potential classic." —**Associated Press**

Summary: Golden Richards, husband to four wives, father to twenty-eight children, is having the mother of all midlife crises. His construction business is failing, his family has grown into an overpopulated mini-dukedom beset with insurrection and rivalry, and he is done in with grief: due to the accidental death of a daughter and the stillbirth of a son, he has come to doubt the capacity of his own heart. Brady Udall, one of our finest American fiction writers, tells a tragicomic story of a deeply faithful man who, crippled by grief and the demands of work and family, becomes entangled in an affair that threatens to destroy his family's future. Like John Irving and Richard Yates, Udall creates characters that engage us to the fullest as they grapple with the nature of need, love, and belonging.

About the Author: **Brady Udall** is the author of *Letting Loose the Hounds*, and *The Miracle Life of Edgar Mint*. His work has appeared in *The Paris Review*, *Esquire*, *Playboy*, and elsewhere. He lives in Boise, Idaho.

CONVERSATION STARTERS

1. What were your views on polygamy before reading the book? Did they change after you finished reading?

2. Discuss Golden's progression from lonely polygamist to social polygamist. How does a renewal of faith assist this transformation?

3. Compare and contrast Golden's behavior at the two funerals. How are they similar? In what ways are they different?

4. How does Glory affect the other family members and Golden in particular?

5. Discuss the motifs of creation and destruction that appear throughout the novel.

6. Do you think Rusty is a representative figure for all of the Richards children in the novel, or is he in some ways unique?

7. Trish is one of the most conflicted mothers in the novel. What do you think of her decision at the end? Was it the right thing to do?

8. How has the family changed at the conclusion of the novel? Do you think they are happy with their decisions?

9. Discuss Rose-of-Sharon's reaction to Rusty's accident. Do you think you would have reacted the same way if you were in her place?

10. Why do you think Golden isn't able to consummate his affair with Huila?

11. Physical appearance is described with exacting clarity throughout the novel. Golden is described as bucktoothed and "Sasquatch," and Glory as "lopsided" and "overstuffed." Why do you think there is such a heightened awareness of the body?

12. What is the effect of polygamy on the women in the novel? How do you think their lives and personalities would be different if they weren't in a polygamous relationship?

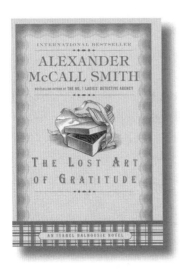

THE LOST ART OF GRATITUDE
An Isabel Dalhousie Novel

AUTHOR: *Alexander McCall Smith*

PUBLISHER: Anchor Books, 2010

WEBSITE: www.ReadingGroupCenter.com
www.alexandermccallsmith.com

AVAILABLE IN: Trade Paperback
288 pages, $14.00, ISBN 978-0307387080

ALSO AVAILABLE AS: eBook

SUBJECTS: Mystery/Women's Lives/Family
(Fiction)

"McCall Smith has created a world where humor is gentle. . . . It's a wonderful place to visit, even if we don't get to live there." —**The Washington Post**

SUMMARY: Isabel's son, Charlie, is now of an age—eighteen months—to have a social life, and so off they go to a birthday party, where, much to Isabel's surprise, she encounters an old adversary, Minty Auchterlonie, now a high-flying financier. Minty had seemed to Isabel a woman of ruthless ambition, but the question of her integrity had never been answered. Now, when Minty takes Isabel into her confidence about a personal matter, Isabel finds herself going another round: Is Minty to be trusted? Or is she the perpetrator of an enormous financial fraud? And what should Isabel make of the rumors of shady financial transactions at Minty's investment bank?

Not that this is the only dilemma facing Isabel: she also crosses swords again with her nemesis, Professor Dove, in an argument over plagiarism. Of course her niece, Cat, has a new, problematic man (a tightrope walker!) in her life. And there remains the open question of marriage to Jamie—doting father of Charlie.

ABOUT THE AUTHOR: **Alexander McCall Smith** is the author of the international phenomenon The No. 1 Ladies' Detective Agency series. He is professor emeritus of medical law at the University of Edinburgh in Scotland and has served on many national and international bodies concerned with bioethics.

CONVERSATION STARTERS

1. Why is this novel called "The Lost Art of Gratitude"? Who is, or should be, grateful? Why is it a lost art?

2. One of Isabel's guiding principles is "moral proximity": If someone you know is in trouble, you must try to help—a notion that Jamie seems to consider meddling. In what ways does this make Isabel's life more fulfilling? And more difficult? What do you think Isabel gets out of this?

3. On page 15, Isabel muses about her life: "She used to think that her major achievement in life had been the editing of the *Review*, or perhaps her doctorate; she no longer thought so—now she felt that the most important thing she had done was to give birth to a whole new life, a whole new set of possibilities." What does this say about her as a philosopher? As a mother?

4. "Perfect villains have to live somewhere, and even the most innocent-looking suburb can conceal its surprises" (p. 21). How does this notion play out over the course of the novel? Is there a perfect villain within Isabel's circle?

5. What role does money play in the novel? How does Minty's wealth affect the way Isabel deals with her? Are there other instances in which money affects characters' behavior?

6. "Stoicism and defeatism, of course, can be kissing cousins, but Isabel would never find fault in Jamie's quite exceptional ability to accept setbacks" (p. 47). What does this tell us about Isabel and Jamie's relationship? How does Isabel respond to setbacks? Is this a function of the difference in their ages?

7. Isabel thinks quite a bit about Scotland, almost as if it were a character in its own right. What point is Alexander McCall Smith trying to make?

8. Discuss the plagiarism subplot. What purpose does it serve? What does Isabel's handling of the situation tell us about her character?

9. Two of Isabel's acquaintances refer to Minty as "wicked" (p. 181). Do you agree with that assessment? Ultimately, does Isabel?

10. Discuss Isabel's relationship with Cat. How does Isabel treat her niece? What does she expect from her?

11. Reread the song lyrics on page 261. How do they reflect upon the events of the novel? What does the song say about Jamie's feelings toward Isabel?

MAJOR PETTIGREW'S LAST STAND

AUTHOR: *Helen Simonson*

PUBLISHER: Random House Trade Paperbacks, December 2010

WEBSITE: www.atrandom.com
www.helensimonson.com

AVAILABLE IN: Trade Paperback
384 pages, $15.00, ISBN 978-0812981223

ALSO AVAILABLE AS: eBook and Audiobook

SUBJECTS: Relationships/Women's Lives/ Cultural & World Issues (Fiction)

"This irresistibly delightful, thoughtful, and utterly charming and surprising novel reads like the work of a seasoned pro. In fact, it is Simonson's debut. One cannot wait to see what she does next."
—*Library Journal*, **starred review**

SUMMARY: Major Pettigrew is one of the most indelible characters in contemporary fiction, and from the very first page of this remarkable novel he will steal your heart. The Major leads a quiet life valuing the proper things that Englishmen have lived by for generations: honor, duty, decorum, and a properly brewed cup of tea. But then his brother's death sparks an unexpected friendship with Mrs. Jasmina Ali, the Pakistani shopkeeper from the village. Drawn together by their shared love of literature and the loss of their respective spouses, the Major and Mrs. Ali soon find their friendship blossoming into something more. But village society insists on embracing him as the quintessential local and her as the permanent foreigner. Can their relationship survive the risks one takes when pursuing happiness in the face of culture and tradition?

ABOUT THE AUTHOR: **Helen Simonson** was born in England but has lived in America for the last two decades. A longtime resident of Brooklyn, she now lives with her husband and two sons in the Washington, D.C., area. This is her first novel.

CONVERSATION STARTERS

1. In the outset of *Major Pettigrew's Last Stand,* the Major is described as feeling the weight of his age, but on page 320, the morning after his romantic evening with Mrs. Ali at Colonel Preston's Lodge, Simonson writes that "a pleasant glow, deep in his gut, was all that remained of a night that seemed to have burned away the years from his back." Love is not only for the young and, as it did the Major, it has the capacity to revitalize. Discuss the agelessness of love, and how it can transform us at any point in our lives.

2. A crucial theme of *Major Pettigrew's Last Stand* is that of obligation. What are the differences between the Pettigrews' familial expectations and those of the Alis'? What do different characters in the novel have to sacrifice in order to stay true to these obligations? What do they give up in diverging from them?

3. Major Pettigrew clings to the civility of a bygone era, and his discussions with Mrs. Ali over tea are a narrative engine of the book and play a central role in their burgeoning romance. In our digital world, how have interpersonal relationships changed? Do you think instant communication makes us more or less in touch with the people around us?

4. Much of the novel focuses on the notion of "otherness." Who is considered an outsider in Edgecombe St. Mary? How are the various village outsiders treated differently?

5. First impressions in *Major Pettigrew's Last Stand* can be deceiving. Discuss the progressions of the characters you feel changed the most from the beginning of the book to the end.

6. Major Pettigrew and Mrs. Ali connect emotionally in part because they share the experience of having lost a spouse, and in part because they delight in love having come around a second time. How do you think relationships formed in grief are different from those that are not?

7. For Major Pettigrew, the Churchills represent societal standing and achievement, as well as an important part of his family's history. However, as events unfold, the Major begins to question whether loyalty and honor are more important than material objects and social status. Discuss the evolving importance of the guns to the Major, as well as the challenge of passing down important objects, and values, to younger generations.

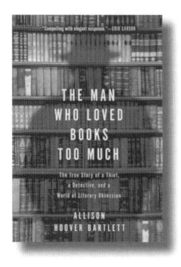

THE MAN WHO LOVED BOOKS TOO MUCH

The True Story of a Thief, a Detective, and a World of Literary Obsession

AUTHOR: *Allison Hoover Bartlett*

PUBLISHER: Riverhead Books, 2010

WEBSITE: www.penguin.com
www.allisonhooverbartlett.com

AVAILABLE IN: Trade Paperback
288 pages, $15.00, ISBN 978-1594484810

ALSO AVAILABLE AS: eBook

SUBJECTS: Literature/Intrigue/History
(Nonfiction)

"A fascinating journey into a strange, obsessive world where a love for books can sometimes become a fatal attraction." —**Simon Worrall, author of** *The Poet and The Murderer*

SUMMARY: **Rare-book theft is even more widespread than fine-art theft. Most thieves, of course, steal for profit. John Charles Gilkey steals purely for the love of books. In an attempt to understand him better, journalist Allison Hoover Bartlett plunged herself into the world of book lust and discovered just how dangerous it can be.**

Gilkey is an obsessed, unrepentant book thief who has stolen hundreds of thousands of dollars' worth of rare books from book fairs, stores, and libraries around the country. Ken Sanders is the self-appointed "bibliodick" (book dealer with a penchant for detective work) driven to catch him. Bartlett befriended both men and found herself caught in the middle of efforts to recover the hidden treasure. With a mixture of suspense, insight, and humor, she weaves an entertaining cat-and-mouse chase into a narrative that not only reveals exactly how Gilkey pulled off his dirtiest crimes, where he stashed the loot, and how Sanders ultimately caught him, but also explores the romance of books, the lure to collect them, and the temptation to steal them.

ABOUT THE AUTHOR: **Allison Hoover Bartlett**'s work has appeared in *The New York Times*, *The Washington Post*, and the *San Francisco Chronicle*, among others. She lives in San Francisco with her husband and two children.

CONVERSATION STARTERS

1. What are the subtleties of stealing for profit versus stealing out of a love for books themselves? Is one more justified than the other?

2. What motivates Bartlett's quest to uncover the stories behind the high profile book thefts? How does this motivation change over the course of the book? Did you find yourself at times sympathizing with or feeling pity for Gilkey? Why or why not?

3. Why do people collect books? What makes certain titles more valuable? The author notes that our books are often "repositories for memories" (p. 20), so given that criteria, what might be your most "valuable" books, and why?

4. Has learning some of the tricks of the book collecting trade—smelling books for signs of mildew encroachment, the flawed nature of "certificates of authenticity," the joy of finding fore-edged paintings— altered or newly inspired your relationship to books? What insights from this story have had the most impact on you and your collection?

5. Why do some collectors (like Gilkey) risk it all—fortune, freedom, and reputation—to steal to add to their collections? What might prevent others, though equally obsessive, from acting in the same way?

6. Why is Gilkey so eager to share his story, including his motivations and theft strategy, with Bartlett? Though it would only increase his profile and make it harder for him to remain anonymous as a thief, what does he stand to gain by telling all?

7. The Northern California bookselling community is a highly unique and close-knit group. Do you think another merchant group could be capable or willing to go to the lengths that they do to catch a serial thief? Why might they have felt so compelled to act, outside of the monetary loss? What is lost if they fail?

8. What ultimately drives Ken Sanders to take on the crusade to nail Gilkey? How would you answer the author who seeks to understand why Gilkey is "so passionate about books . . . he would put his freedom on the line for them" and why Sanders is "so determined to catch him . . . [he'd put] the financial stability of his store on the line for it"?

9. Do you think Bartlett had an ethical obligation to share the details Gilkey revealed to her with the authorities or other booksellers? Do you agree with her rationalization as she shifted "from an observer to participant in Gilkey's story" (p. 241)?

MY ABANDONMENT

AUTHOR: *Peter Rock*

PUBLISHER: Mariner Books, 2010

WEBSITE: www.hmhbooks.com

AVAILABLE IN: Trade Paperback
240 pages, $13.95, ISBN 978-0156035521

ALSO AVAILABLE AS: eBook and Audiobook

SUBJECTS: Family/Personal Challenges/
Environment & Nature (Fiction)

"This beautiful, strange novel takes us into the foreign country where those called homeless are at home, the city is wilderness, and the greater wilderness lies beyond. Fascinating and moving, it tells with great tenderness how human love goes wrong."
—**Ursula K. Le Guin**

SUMMARY: A thirteen-year-old girl and her father live in Forest Park, an enormous nature preserve in Portland, Oregon. They inhabit an elaborate cave shelter, wash in a nearby creek, store perishables at the water's edge, use a makeshift septic system, tend a garden, even keep a library of sorts. Once a week they go to the city to buy groceries and otherwise merge with the civilized world. But one small mistake allows a backcountry jogger to discover them, which derails their entire existence, ultimately provoking a deeper flight. Inspired by a true story and told through the startlingly sincere voice of its young narrator, Caroline, *My Abandonment* is a riveting journey into life at the margins and a mesmerizing tale of survival and hope.

ABOUT THE AUTHOR: **Peter Rock** is an Associate Professor of Creative Writing at Reed College in Portland, Oregon. He has been with Reed College since 2001. Peter Rock was born and raised in Salt Lake City, Utah. He is the author of the novels *The Unsettling*, *The Bewildered*, *The Ambidextrist*, *This is the Place*, and *Carnival Wolves*.

CONVERSATION STARTERS

1. When the book opens, Caroline and Father are scavenging scrap metal from a junk yard. "'You see, Caroline,' Father says, 'all the work I'm doing here for these people, organizing all these different things. This is how we are paying them back for what we're taking'" (p. 4). Why is it important to Father to "pay back" for what they take? Is Father concerned with morality? Can you find other examples where he justifies an action that others might think is wrong? How does Caroline see Father's actions? Does the way Caroline judges Father change over the course of the book?

2. On page 14, Father says, " 'Beware of all enterprises that require new clothes.' " This is a quotation from Thoreau's *Walden*. Father quotes from Thoreau and two other writers throughout; at the end of the book, Caroline discovers who they are. How are your feelings about Father affected by knowing what he's reading and thinking about? Do you think that Caroline and Father are living a sort of Thoreauvian idyll in the early pages of the book? Is it more difficult to go "back to the land" now than it was in Thoreau's day?

3. If Caroline and Father are living in a kind of natural, innocent state at the beginning of the book, that all changes when their home is discovered. What is the incident that precedes their being discovered? Is this "fall from grace" Caroline's fault? Why or why not?

4. At the end of chapter six, Caroline tells how she and Father came to be together. What do you think of this story, and of how Caroline tells it? Is she a reliable narrator? "'If I weren't your father,' he says, 'how could I have walked right into your backyard and walked away with you and no one said a word?'" (p. 191). Does this story change the way you feel about Father?

5. At the end of the book, Caroline is living alone in an eight-sided yurt. "Father and I are a family of writers" (p. 223), she says, and she is writing the story of her life: "all my piles of papers and artifacts from all the times, how I have broken it down to organize my story and be able to tell it . . . eight piles, one for each wall" (pp. 221–222). Caroline has structured her story the way she has "constructed" her house; she's almost literally living inside her story. And, of course, the eight chapters of Caroline's story are the eight chapters of *My Abandonment*. Think about these two uses of "structure" or "constructed." In what way do we all construct the stories of our lives? How do we live in our own stories?

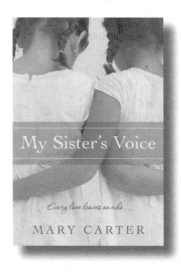

MY SISTER'S VOICE

Author: *Mary Carter*

Publisher: Kensington Trade Paperback, 2010

Website: www.kensingtonbooks.com
www.marycarterbooks.com

Available in: Trade Paperback
336 pages, $15.00, ISBN 978-0758229205

Also Available as: eBook

Subjects: Family/Relationships/
Personal Challenges (Fiction)

"Gripping, entertaining and honest. This is a unique, sincere story about the invisible, unbreakable bonds of sisterhood that sustain us no matter how far they're buried." —**Cathy Lamb, author of *Henry's Sisters* and *Julia's Chocolates***

Summary: At twenty-eight, Laccy Gears is exactly where she wants to be. An up-and-coming, proudly Deaf artist in Philadelphia, she's in a relationship with a wonderful man and rarely thinks about her difficult childhood in a home for disabled orphans. That is, until Lacey receives a letter that begins, "You have a sister. A twin to be exact..."

Learning that her identical, hearing twin, Monica, experienced the normal childhood she was denied resurrects all of Lacey's grief, and she angrily sets out to find Monica and her biological parents. But the truth about Monica's life, their brief shared past, and the reason for the twins' separation is far from simple. And for every one of Lacey's questions that's answered, others are raised, more baffling and profound.

Complex, moving, and beautifully told, *My Sister's Voice* is a novel about sisterhood, love of every shape, and the stories we cling to until real life comes crashing in.

About the Author: **Mary Carter** lives and writes in New York City where she is currently working on a new novel.

CONVERSATION STARTERS

1. How are Monica and Lacey alike? How are they different?
2. How does Lacey feel about being Deaf? What kind of discrimination or misconceptions about deafness does she face?
3. Do you think Lacey would have reacted differently to Monica if they were biological sisters but not identical twins? If yes, how so, and why?
4. What do the professions chosen by Lacey and Monica say about their personalities? In what ways is each successful in her career, and in what ways has each been holding back?
5. Who do you think had the worse childhood? Why?
6. Was one twin betrayed more than the other by their parents? If yes, which twin?
7. What role do secrets play in the book? Which twin is more likely to keep secrets?
8. If Monica had been sent away and Lacey raised by Richard and Katherine, do you believe Monica would have had the same reaction to being given up that Lacey had?
9. Which twin is the happiest?
10. Would Lacey have the same personality if she were hearing?
11. Would Monica have the same personality if she were Deaf?
12. Do you understand Katherine's decision to give Lacey up? Why or why not? Was Richard a passive voice in the decision, or an active participant? Does it make him more or less responsible?
13. Would Monica have stayed with Joe if she had never met Lacey?
14. Would Lacey and Alan have parted ways if Lacey had never met Monica?
15. What influence did Aunt Grace have on Monica's life? On Lacey's?
16. Besides speaking and signing, what methods does Lacey employ to communicate with hearing people?
17. Which twin is more jealous of the other?
18. If they had been raised together, would one twin have overshadowed the other? If yes, which twin and why?
19. Will Monica and Lacey ever confront all the family secrets, or will they perpetuate the cycle?
20. Is it normal for Lacey to want a deaf child?
21. Which has had more influence on the twins: nature or nurture? Which commonalities prove or disprove either side of the debate?
22. Which twin changes the most by the end of the book?

NOTHING WAS THE SAME

AUTHOR: *Kay Redfield Jamison*

PUBLISHER: Vintage Books, January 2011

WEBSITE: www.ReadingGroupCenter.com

AVAILABLE IN: Trade Paperback
224 pages, $14.95, ISBN 978-0307277893

ALSO AVAILABLE AS: eBook

SUBJECTS: Biography/Family/Relationships
(Memoir)

"The great gift Jamison offers here, beyond her honesty and the beauty of her writing, is perspective: a clear-eyed view of illness and death, sanity and insanity, love and grief."—**Reeve Lindbergh,** *The Washington Post*

SUMMARY: Wyatt was forty-five and Jamison thirty-eight when they met in 1985. For nearly twenty years, they delighted in their love for each other, their shared interest in science and medicine, and the knowledge that each had been given a second chance at life. Wyatt saw Jamison through the mercurial moods of her illness and fully supported her decision to tell the truth about her life in *An Unquiet Mind.* Their professional lives were productive and often hectic, their personal lives filled with romantic vacations, Wyatt's charmingly outlandish gestures of love, intensely satisfying physical affection, and quiet moments of reading and conversation. Both seemed to be enjoying good health until 1999, when Wyatt was diagnosed with lung cancer. Despite cutting-edge medical procedures, he died in the spring of 2002.

Nothing Was the Same celebrates the many different ways love is expressed and reveals how it survives painful situations and loss.

ABOUT THE AUTHOR: **Kay Redfield Jamison** is the author of the national best sellers *An Unquiet Mind* and *Night Falls Fast,* as well as *Exuberance* and *Touched with Fire.* She is the recipient of numerous national and international scientific awards and of a John D. and Catherine T. MacArthur Fellowship.

CONVERSATION STARTERS

1. How does the prologue set the stage for Jamison's investigation into grief? What does it convey about the narrative method she has chosen to employ? Does her expertise as a psychologist color her description of her immediate reaction to her husband's death?

2. What personality traits contributed to Wyatt's ability to deal with dyslexia? How did the circumstances of his childhood affect not only his intellectual development but also his ambition and choice of career? Does his experience with dyslexia both as a child and an adult provide insight into learning disabilities and how they are generally perceived?

3. What emotional and intellectual factors play a role in Wyatt's response to Jamison's illness, as well as his mechanisms for dealing with troubling incidents? What does his decision to keep antipsychotic medication at hand demonstrate about the conflicting pulls of trust and uncertainty in their marriage? Are Jamison's feelings of betrayal justified? Does Wyatt's response—"I am imperfect. . . . You are imperfect. . . . Love is imperfect"—define the foundation of successful marriages and relationships?

4. What do her trips to California represent to Jamison? In what ways do they reflect her inner journey and her acceptance of the inevitability of Wyatt's death?

5. "I realized that it was not that I didn't want to go on without him. I did. It was just that I didn't *why* I wanted to go on. It would have to be an act of faith." Talk about how memories of Wyatt, the consolations of friends, and Jamison's ability to imagine "a different way of being together" all help sustain her during the early days after Wyatt's death. What other resources does she draw upon?

6. Are Wyatt's and Jamison's attitudes influenced by their ability to take advantage of medical advice and breakthroughs not available to others? What does their story demonstrate about America's medical system? What does it reveal about the possibilities, as well as the limitations, of modern medicine?

7. If you have read *An Unquiet Mind*, in what respects is *Nothing Was the Same* a sequel? What themes or message emerge in both books? In what ways has Jamison changed in the years since *An Unquiet Mind* and what accounts for those changes?

8. Does *Nothing Was the Same* transcend Jamison's personal story to illuminate the universal experience of grief? What practical guidance and emotional insights does the book offer to readers?

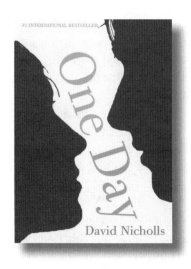

ONE DAY

AUTHOR: *David Nicholls*

PUBLISHER: Vintage Books, 2010

WEBSITE: www.ReadingGroupCenter.com
www.davidnichollswriter.com

AVAILABLE IN: Trade Paperback
448 pages, $14.95, ISBN 978-0307474711

ALSO AVAILABLE AS: eBook and Audiobook

SUBJECTS: Relationships/Coming of Age/
Identity (Fiction)

"A big, absorbing, smart, fantastically readable on-off love story."
—**Nick Hornby, from his blog**

*"[An] instant classic. . . . One of the most hilarious and emotionally riveting love stories you'll ever encounter." —**People***

SUMMARY: Emma Morley and Dexter Mayhew, casual acquaintances during their university years, spend graduation night together. It's July 15, 1988, and their futures are up in the air. Dexter, the handsome, confident son of a well-to-do family, knows only that he wants "to be successful. . . . to live life to the extreme, but without any mess or complications" [p. 9]. Emma is determined to stay true to her left-leaning passions and ideals though she has little idea of how she'll do it. They part the next day with vague promises to keep in touch as Dexter sets off to travel the world and Emma returns to her working-class family in Leeds to figure out what she'll do next. Over the next twenty years, they'll think about each other, sometimes to meet and reignite a relationship that neither can give up nor explain. David Nicholls brilliantly explores the interplay of character and fate that shape our lives.

ABOUT THE AUTHOR: **David Nicholls** is the author of the novels *Starter for Ten* and *The Understudy*. He wrote an adaptation of *Tess of the D'Urbervilles* for the BBC and has written several other screenplays.

CONVERSATION STARTERS

1. To what extent do Emma's thoughts and assumptions about Dexter [pp. 5–6] and Dexter's sketch of Emma [pp. 8-9] rely on facile stereotypes they each harbor? In what ways do they embody more measured reflections? How accurate are their assessments?

2. What determines the path Emma follows in her post-university years? In addition to being a wonderfully comic interlude, how does her stint with Sledgehammer Theater Cooperative enrich the portrait of the time in which the novel is set? Is Emma's explanation of why she ended up working at the tacky Mexican restaurant—"there was a recession on and people were clinging to their jobs. . . . the government had ended student grants" [p. 56]—honest?

3. Does Dexter's meteoric rise in television change the fundamental dynamics between Dexter and Emma? What aspects of their relationship remain unchanged? What influences the things they say and, perhaps more importantly, what they don't say, during their afternoon on Primrose Hill [p. 60–72]? Who is more aware of—and affected by—the sexual tensions and temptations they both experience?

4. When he meets Sylvie Cope, Dexter thinks, "And yet, despite all this, the downturn in professional fortunes, he is fine now, because he has fallen in love with Sylvie, beautiful Sylvie. . . ." [p. 251]. In what ways does the affair open Dexter's eyes to new possibilities and a different way of life? What flaws in their relationship does he fail to grasp fully and why?

5. Callum is casually mentioned as mutual friend in Chapter 2 [p. 21] and chapter 6 [p. 109] and Ian makes his first appearance simply as Emma's co-worker in Chapter 3 [p. 37]; both will become significant figures. What other secondary characters become more important than the protagonists—and the reader—anticipate? What do these "surprises" reflect about the way lives unfold?

6. What does *One Day* share with traditional boy-meets-girl stories you are familiar with from books or movies? What does it suggest about the relationship between love and happiness?

7. Throughout the novel, Dexter and Emma withhold or suppress their feeling for one another. Is one of them more guilty of this and, if so, why? What role does fate (e.g. Dexter's unsent letter, missed phone calls, etc.), along with the characters' assumptions and misinterpretations, play in the plot?

THE PATTERN IN THE CARPET
A Personal History with Jigsaws

AUTHOR: *Margaret Drabble*

PUBLISHER: Mariner Books, 2010

WEBSITE: www.marinerbooks.com
www.redmood.com/drabble

AVAILABLE IN: Trade Paperback
368 pages, $14.95, ISBN 978-0547386096

ALSO AVAILABLE AS: eBook

SUBJECTS: Biography/Family/Relationships
(Memoir)

"One of a kind. . . . It will take the reader on a journey unlike anything else in the bookstore." —**Christian Science Monitor**

SUMMARY: *The Pattern in the Carpet: A Personal History with Jigsaws* is an original and brilliant work. Margaret Drabble weaves her own story into a history of games, in particular jigsaws, which have offered her and many others relief from melancholy and depression. Alongside curious facts and discoveries about jigsaw puzzles—did you know that the 1929 stock market crash was followed by a boom in puzzle sales?—Drabble introduces us to her beloved Auntie Phyl, and describes childhood visits to the house in Long Bennington on the Great North Road, their first trip to London together, the books they read, and the jigsaws they completed. She offers penetrating sketches of her parents, siblings, and children, and shares her thoughts on the importance of childhood play, on art and writing, and on aging and memory. And she does so with her customary intelligence, energy, and wit. This is a memoir like no other.

ABOUT THE AUTHOR: **Margaret Drabble** is the author of *The Sea Lady*, *The Seven Sisters*, *The Peppered Moth*, and *The Needle's Eye*, among other novels. She is the editor of the fifth and sixth editions of *The Oxford Companion to English Literature*. For her contributions to contemporary English literature, she was made a Dame of the British Empire in 2008.

CONVERSATION STARTERS

1. In the Introduction, Drabble begins the book by saying it is not a memoir, though it might look like one. What are the implications of this statement? What sorts of expectations do we bring to a memoir? How does this book defy or fulfill those expectations?

2. Drabble writes that the book is not a history of jigsaw puzzles, "though that is what it was once meant to be." Throughout the text, Drabble makes occasional references to the writing of the book, breaking the narrative voice to speak directly to the reader and call attention to the book itself. Why does she do this? What did you think of these authorial asides and interruptions?

3. On page 12, Drabble states, "I am not very good at jigsaws. That is one of the reasons why I like them so much." Does this statement surprise you? Do you enjoy tasks that you're not particularly accomplished at? What can be gained by doing a pastime that is difficult for you?

4. The book begins and ends with Auntie Phyl. What role did Auntie Phyl play in the author's life?

5. In Chapter XXVIII, Drabble notes that when she was younger, she assumed that psychological pain would recede as one grew older, eclipsed by physical pain. "That's what I used to think, or fear, or hope" (p. 171). Later on she says, "At times I feel some pride in my continuing capacity for feeling really, really bad" (p. 172). What do you think Drabble means by that? Why would she feel pride in her suffering?

6. Death is always nearby in Drabble's book—Auntie Phyl's, her mother's, and her own. Jigsaws are presented sometimes as merely a diversion to pass the time until death. But the book ends with a comment on books themselves, and the effort of writing them: "Books, too, have beginnings and endings, and they attempt to impose a pattern, to make a shape. We aim, by writing them, to make order from chaos. We fail. The admission of failure is the best we can do. It is a form of progress" (p. 338). What do you think of these words, from a writer toward the end of her life? Do you imagine a younger writer would agree? Do you agree?

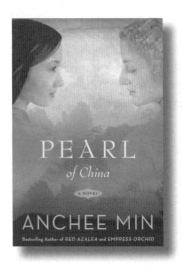

PEARL OF CHINA

AUTHOR: *Anchee Min*

PUBLISHER: Bloomsbury USA, 2010

WEBSITE: www.bloomsburyusa.com
www.ancheemin.com

AVAILABLE IN: Hardcover
288 pages, $24.00, ISBN 978-1596916975

ALSO AVAILABLE AS: eBook

SUBJECTS: History/Women's Issues/
Culture and World Issues (Fiction)

"Min's fresh and penetrating interpretation of Pearl S. Buck's extraordinary life delivers profound psychological, spiritual, and historical insights within an unforgettable cross-cultural story of a quest for veracity, compassion, and justice." —**Booklist (starred review)**

SUMMARY: Willow never dreamed that her childhood friend would become a world-renowned writer. In the impoverished Chinese village of Chinkiang, a young pickpocket meets her match in Pearl Sydenstricker, the daughter of the village's only white man, a Christian missionary named Absalom. Willow and her Papa befriend Pearl's family to get a hot meal, but eventually Papa and Absalom become partners in recruiting the villagers to join the church. Meanwhile, Willow and Pearl strike up a friendship that will last a lifetime. As Willow and Pearl come of age, their lives diverge: Willow is forced to become a concubine, and Pearl leaves Chin-kiang to study in Shanghai and America. When Pearl returns to the village, it is to marry Lossing Buck, an ambitious American agriculturist.

ABOUT THE AUTHOR: **Anchee Min** was born in Shanghai in 1957. Her first book, the memoir *Red Azalea*, became an international bestseller. She has also published five previous novels: *Empress Orchid* and *The Last Empress*, set during the last years of Imperial China; and *Katherine, Becoming Madame Mao*, and *Wild Ginger*, set during the Cultural Revolution and its aftermath. Her books have been translated into thirty-two languages.

CONVERSATION STARTERS

1. *Pearl of China* opens with a quotation from Pearl S. Buck: "I was never deceived by Chinese women, not even by the flower-like lovely girls. They are the strongest women in the world." Discuss how two strong-willed characters in *Pearl of China*, Willow and Madame Mao, display the fortitude that Buck describes. How are these two women's strengths similar and different? Who benefits—and who suffers—from these two women's powers?

2. Describe the changing fortune of Willow's family. When we first meet Willow, how is her family coping with poverty? How do their fortunes change over the course of the novel? How does Willow's peasant background eventually become an advantage?

3. Although Pearl is American, "beneath her skin, she was Chinese." (263) What Chinese qualities does Pearl exhibit in childhood and in adulthood? What American characteristics does she have? How is Pearl able to reconcile her Chinese heritage and her Western birth?

4. How does the church endure and evolve after Absalom's death?

5. Marital problems plague many characters in *Pearl of China*. Consider the following troubled couples: Absalom and Carie, Pearl and Lossing, Willow and Dick. What do these marriages have in common, and how are they different? What better models of love and coupling exist within the novel?

6. Discuss the theme of forgiveness in *Pearl of China*. When are Papa, Dick, and Bumpkin Emperor forgiven, and why? What friendships and values are strengthened through forgiveness? Which characters have difficulty forgiving others' transgressions, and why?

7. As she begins to write novels, Pearl tells Willow, "The character must believe in himself, and he must have the stamina to endure." (113) Does Willow display the courage that Pearl describes? What hardships is Willow able to endure? At which moments is her belief in herself especially challenged?

8. Willow reminisces, "Without Pearl and Hsu Chih-mo in my life, I never would have been the person I am today . . . Although I published and impressed others as a writer, it was never my air and rice, as it was for Pearl and Hsu Chih-mo." (155–56) How does writing serve as "air and rice" for Pearl and Hsu Chih-mo? How do Pearl and Willow maintain their connection to Hsu Chih-mo after his death?

9. If you have read *The Good Earth*, discuss similarities and differences between Buck's novel and Min's *Pearl of China*. How does each author portray the people, land, and troubles of rural China?

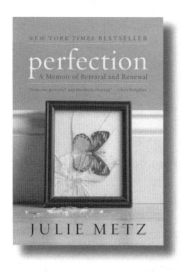

PERFECTION
A Memoir of Betrayal and Renewal

AUTHOR: *Julie Metz*

PUBLISHER: Voice, 2010

WEBSITE: www.everywomansvoice.com
www.perfectionbook.com

AVAILABLE IN: Trade Paperback
352 pages, $14.99, ISBN 978-1401341350

ALSO AVAILABLE AS: eBook

SUBJECTS: Identity/Personal Discovery/
Women's Lives (Memoir)

"Metz's Perfection *chronicles with lapidary precision one woman's climb back to happiness after not just a spouse's death, but also the shocking recognition that her life before that death was not what she had thought it was. The journey is a painful one, but Ms. Metz is much the stronger for having survived to recount it."* —**Julie Powell, author of** *Julie & Julia*

SUMMARY: Julie Metz's life changes forever on one ordinary January afternoon when her husband, Henry, collapses on the kitchen floor and dies in her arms. Suddenly, this mother of a six-year-old is the young widow in a bucolic small town. And this is only the beginning. Seven months after Henry's death, just when Julie thinks she is emerging from the worst of it, comes the rest of it: She discovers that what had appeared to be the reality of her marriage was but a half-truth. Henry had hidden another life from her.

Perfection is the story of Julie Metz's journey through chaos and trans-formation as she creates a different life for herself and her young daughter. It is the story of coming to terms with painful truths, of rebuilding both a life and an identity after betrayal and widowhood. It is a story of rebirth and happiness—if not perfection,

ABOUT THE AUTHOR: **Julie Metz** is a writer whose essays have appeared in publications including *Glamour* and *Hemispheres* magazines, and the online story site mrbellersneighborhood.com.

CONVERSATION STARTERS

1. How does the author's voice change as the book progresses? What does that tell the reader about her emotional state?

2. How does the book's structure show the changes Julie experiences?

3. Have you ever witnessed a death, lived through the death of a person close to you, or watched a friend or relative cope with grief? How do your experiences compare to Julie's? How do you think our culture copes with death?

4. What is the symbolism of food throughout the book? What did food mean to Henry? What does it mean to Julie and to her daughter Liza? What does umami mean to you?

5. The events in this story take place in a small town. How does this environment affect Julie? How does she respond to other environments in the book: France, Italy, Maine, and New York City? What is the impact of your own environment on your life? What role does travel play in the healing process?

6. Have you experienced betrayal in a relationship? How did you cope with this? If you have not experienced this directly, how do you think you might cope?

7. How do you feel about the relationships Julie has after Henry's death?

8. How is Julie's sense of family affected by Henry's death? How does this understanding of family change?

9. How does Julie's definition of love change over the course of the book? How do you define love?

10. What do you make of Professor Symons' evolutionary analysis of human mating behavior? How do you see the differences between men and women?

11. Do you think that times of crisis have their hidden benefits? What do you think Julie learns from her experiences? How does it affect her life as a woman, mother, and artist?

12. What do you think are the various meanings of the title? What does the word "Perfection" mean to you?

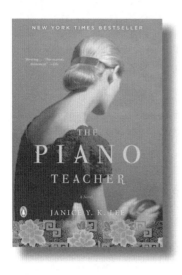

THE PIANO TEACHER

Author: *Janice Y. K. Lee*

Publisher: Penguin Books, 2009

Website: www.penguingroup.com
www.janiceyklee.com

Available in: Trade Paperback
336 pages, $15.00, ISBN 978-0143116530

Also Available as: eBook and Audiobook

Subjects: History/Women's Lives/
Culture & World Issues (Fiction)

"War, love, betrayal—an exquisite fugue of a first novel. . . . Intensely readable." —**O, The Oprah Magazine**

"Sleek, spare prose. . . . The Piano Teacher *is laced with intrigue."*
—**New York Times Book Review**

Summary: Demure and unsophisticated, Claire Pendleton is the quintessential English rose when she first arrives in Hong Kong. The year is 1952 and, as the wife of an English engineer overseeing the construction of a new reservoir, Claire seems destined to lead an insulated life, socializing with the other expatriate wives. But when she takes a position giving piano lessons to Locket Chen, the daughter of a wealthy and powerful local family, she enters a world of deceit, passion, and dark secrets that will deeply shock Hong Kong society and change Claire forever.

About the Author: **Janice Y. K. Lee** was born and raised in Hong Kong and graduated from Harvard College. A former features editor at *Elle* and *Mirabella* magazines, she currently lives in Hong Kong with her husband and children.

CONVERSATION STARTERS

1. Why does Claire steal from the Chens? Why does she stop doing it?

2. Part of Claire's attraction to Will is that he allows her to be someone different than she had always been. Have you ever been drawn to a person or a situation because it offered you the opportunity to reinvent yourself?

3. The amahs are a steady but silent presence throughout the book. Imagine Trudy and Will's relationship and then Claire and Will's affair from their point of view and discuss

4. Trudy was initially drawn to Will because of his quiet equanimity and Will to Claire because of her innocence. Yet those are precisely the qualities each loses in the course of their love affairs. What does this say about the nature of these relationships? Would Will have been attracted to a woman like Claire before Trudy?

5. What is the irony behind Claire's adoration of the young Princess Elizabeth?

6. Were Dominick and Trudy guilty of collaboration, or were they simply trying to survive? Do their circumstances absolve them of their actions?

7. Mary, Tobias's mother, and one of Will's fellow prisoners in Stanley, does not take advantage of her job in the kitchen to steal more food for her son. Yet she prostitutes herself to preserve him. Is Tobias's physical survival worth the psychological damage she's inflicting?

8. Did Trudy give her emerald ring and Locket to Melody? How much did Melody really know?

9. How do Ned Young's experiences parallel Trudy's?

10. Did Will fail Trudy? Was his decision to remain in Stanley rather than be with her on the outside—as he believes—an act of cowardice?

11. Would Locket be better off knowing the truth about her parentage?

12. What would happen if Trudy somehow survived and came back to Will? Could they find happiness together?

THE PILLARS OF THE EARTH

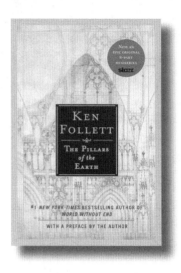

AUTHOR: *Ken Follett*

PUBLISHER: NAL Paperback

WEBSITE: www.penguin.com/pillars
www.ken-follett.com

AVAILABLE IN: Trade Paperback
973 pages, $24.95, ISBN 978-0451225245

ALSO AVAILABLE AS: eBook and Audiobook

SUBJECTS: History/Intrigue/
Culture & World Issues (Fiction)

"A novel of majesty and power." —***Chicago Sun-Times***

"Enormous and brilliant . . . a great epic tale . . . crammed with characters unbelievably alive across the great gulf of centuries . . . touches all human emotion—love and hate, loyalty and treachery, hope and despair. See for yourself. This is truly a novel to get lost in." —***Cosmopolitan***

"An extraordinary epic buttressed by suspense . . . a monumental masterpiece. . . . A towering triumph from a major talent." —***Booklist***

"A seesaw of tension. . . . A novel that entertains, instructs, and satisfies on a grand scale." —***Publishers Weekly***

SUMMARY: The spellbinding epic set in twelfth-century England, *The Pillars of the Earth* tells the story of the lives entwined in the building of the greatest Gothic cathedral the world has ever known—and a struggle between good and evil that will turn church against state, and brother against brother.

ABOUT THE AUTHOR: **Ken Follett** is one of the world's best-loved novelists. He has sold more than one hundred million copies. His recent book, *World Without End*, went straight to the No. 1 position on bestseller lists in the United States, Spain, Italy, Germany, and France. His latest book is *Fall of Giants*.

CONVERSATION STARTERS

1. Ken Follett has said: "When I started to look at cathedrals, I wondered: Who built them, and why? The book is my answer to that question." Why do you think the great medieval cathedrals were built? *Some things to think about*: How does the building of the cathedral satisfy the ambitions of the main characters—Tom Builder, Prior Philip, Aliena, and Jack? How does it affect the lives of other important characters in the story?

2. Read the first scene in Chapter 10 and think about the prose style. Why do you think the author writes this way? Compare the last scene of the same chapter. *Some things to think about*: The number of words of one syllable; the length of sentences; the length of paragraphs; the adjectives used. What is different about the author's purpose in these two scenes?

3. Although *The Pillars of the Earth* is fiction, it includes some real-life characters and incidents from history, such as King Stephen at the battle of Lincoln, and the murder of Thomas Becket. Why does the author mix fact and fiction like this? *Some things to think about*: Are the factual scenes told from the point of view of the real-life characters, or the fictional ones? Are the fictional characters major or minor players in the big historical events of the time?

4. Women were second-class citizens in medieval society and the church. Is this accurately reflected in *The Pillars of the Earth*? *Some things to think about*: What attitudes are shown by Prior Philip and William Hamleigh? How do Agnes, Ellen, and Aliena respond to society's expectations?

5. Some readers have said that they look at medieval churches with new eyes after reading *The Pillars of the Earth*. Do you think you will do the same? *Some things to think about*: In the book, churches are usually viewed through the eyes of a builder. How does this affect your understanding of the architecture?

6. Ken Follett has said: "I'm not a very spiritual person. I'm more interested in the material problems of building a cathedral." Is *The Pillars of the Earth* a spiritual book? *Some things to think about*: What motivates Prior Philip? What does Tom say at the beginning of Chapter 5, when Philip asks him why he wants to be master builder? In Chapter 16, why does Philip ask Remigius to come back to the priory?

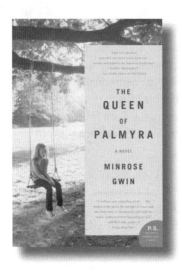

THE QUEEN OF PALMYRA

AUTHOR: *Minrose Gwin*

PUBLISHER: Harper Perennial, 2010

WEBSITE: www.harperperennial.com

AVAILABLE IN: Trade Paperback
416 pages, $14.99, ISBN 978-0061840326

ALSO AVAILABLE AS: eBook

SUBJECTS: History/Social Issues/
Coming of Age (Fiction)

"Here it is, the most powerful and also the most lyrical novel about race, racism, and denial in the American South since To Kill A Mockingbird. *. . . Minrose Gwin tells the story through the voice of Florence Irene Forrest, a girl growing up in a segregated Mississippi community where her father is a secret Klan leader while her main support comes from an African American family. . . .* The Queen of Palmyra *is finally a testament to the ultimate power of truth and knowledge, language and love."*
—**Lee Smith, author of *On Agate Hill***

SUMMARY: In the turbulent southern summer of 1963, Millwood's white population steers clear of "Shake Rag," the black section of town. Young Florence Forrest is one of the few who crosses the line. Florence attaches herself to her grandparents' longtime maid, Zenie Johnson. Named for Zenobia, Queen of Palmyra, Zenie treats the unwanted girl as just another chore, while telling her stories of the legendary queen's courage and cunning.

The more time Florence spends in Shake Rag, the more she recognizes how completely race divides her town, and her story, far from ordinary, bears witness to the truth and brutality of her times

ABOUT THE AUTHOR: **Minrose Gwin** has written three scholarly books and coedited *The Literature of the American South*. She teaches contemporary fiction at UNC–Chapel Hill and, like her young protagonist, grew up in a small Mississippi town.

CONVERSATION STARTERS

1. Why do you think the novel is entitled *The Queen of Palmyra*, named after the legendary Zenobia, who took on the whole empire of Rome—and lost? Is the "queen" of the book one person or several? What does it mean to be a "queen"?

2. "True stories happen and then you tell them. But what you tell depends on what you see. And what you see depends on what you know," Florence Forrest observes in the final pages of the novel. How is seeing dependent on knowing in *The Queen of Palmyra*? How does the novel pivot, as Lee Smith has observed, between seeing and not seeing, knowing and not knowing?

3. "I need you to understand how ordinary it all was." The intimate story of two families, one African American and one white, is played out against a backdrop of the racial tension and unrest that gripped the American South of the 1960s. How does the historical dimension of the story deepen and enhance our sense of everyday life under Jim Crow? How do we find the truth of history in the everyday, the ordinary?

4. The book abounds in stories with competing and contradictory messages: Uncle Wiggily, Br'er Rabbit, Bomba the Swamp Boy, Queen Zenobia. In what sense is the novel about the nature of stories and their multiple, often conflicting functions in human thought and action? What do these stories teach Florence Forrest? What do they tell us about the characters who tell them?

5. Florence's story is interrupted briefly near the end of the book by Eva Greene, who narrates her own murder in excruciating detail. What is the effect of this interruption? What do we learn from Eva in the moment of her death?

6. Why do sentences and diagrams feature so prominently in the novel? What does Florence mean when she says that Eva gave her "the sentence"? Why is it a diagrammed sentence on a blackboard that finally enables Florence to forsake her "willed, necessary blindness" and 'see'?

7. Why, at the end of the book, does Florence take "that sharp left," choosing to return to her own story rather than allowing herself to be swept away by the hurricane as she had planned? What will her life be like now?

THE QUICKENING

AUTHOR: *Michelle Hoover*

PUBLISHER: Other Press, 2010

WEBSITE: www.otherpress.com
www.michellehoover.net

AVAILABLE IN: Trade Paperback
224 pages, $14.95, ISBN 978-1590513460

ALSO AVAILABLE AS: eBook and Audiobook

SUBJECTS: Family/Personal Challenges/
American History (Fiction)

"A vivid, pastoral panorama . . . imbued throughout with a careful and evenly wrought lyricism." —**Kirkus Reviews**

SUMMARY: Enidina Current and Mary Morrow live on neighboring farms in the flat, hard country of the upper Midwest during the early 1900s. This hardscrabble life comes easily to some, like Eddie, who has never wanted more than the land she works and the animals she raises on it with her husband, Frank. But for the deeply religious Mary, farming is an awkward living and at odds with her more cosmopolitan inclinations. Still, Mary creates a clean and orderly home life for her stormy husband, Jack, and her sons, while she adapts to the isolation of a rural town through the inspiration of a local preacher. She is the first to befriend Eddie in a relationship that will prove as rugged as the ground they walk on. Despite having little in common, Eddie and Mary need one another for survival and companionship. But as the Great Depression threatens, the delicate balance of their reliance on one another tips, pitting neighbor against neighbor, exposing the dark secrets they hide from one another, and triggering a series of disquieting events that threaten to unravel not only their friendship but their families as well.

ABOUT THE AUTHOR: **Michelle Hoover**, 2005 the winner of the PEN/New England Discovery Award for Fiction, was born in Ames, Iowa, the granddaughter of four longtime farming families.

CONVERSATION STARTERS

1. Discuss the ways the author uses landscape as a character in *The Quickening*.

2. The tension between Enidina and Mary slowly builds from a personality conflict until it becomes an enduring family feud. In what ways does this evolve from a difference in values? In what ways is it shaped by external forces?

3. As a reader, did you find yourself "taking sides"? Why? Did your allegiances change over the course of the book?

4. How does the novel explore the uneasy relationship between money and morality? In dire financial times, how do the Currents balance the needs of their family and farm, and what they believe is right? What about the Morrows? How are these themes and dilemmas relevant to our own time?

5. Compare Enidina and Frank's marriage to Jack and Mary's. How does their love change over the course of the novel? In each relationship, how do circumstances bring them together? How do they drive them apart?

6. One of the driving forces and major themes of *The Quickening* is betrayal. How does betrayal—real or perceived—shape the relationships between various characters? In which cases do you think the character is right to feel wronged? In which cases do you disagree?

7. Do you think that Enidina and Mary's friendship is entirely one of necessity? After all, the Currents managed fine before the Morrows moved in down the road. If it is, then what kind of necessity? Practical, emotional, financial, familial? How does this change over the course of the novel?

8. How are the children—especially Kyle and Adaline—shaped by the relationship between their mother and father? Between their two families?

9. How does Mary's religious devotion affect her sense of righteousness? Do you believe that she genuinely tries to do the right thing? Or does she, more often, try to convince herself that she has done the |right thing?

10. What do you think the novel says about the possibility and nature of forgiveness? Is redemption possible? Do the characters find it?

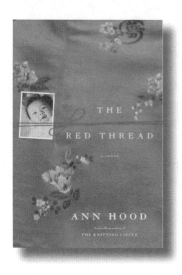

THE RED THREAD

AUTHOR: *Ann Hood*

PUBLISHER: W.W. Norton & Company, Inc, 2010

WEBSITE: www.wwnorton.com
www.annhood.us.com

AVAILABLE IN: Hardcover
304 pages, $23.95,ISBN 978-0393070200

ALSO AVAILABLE AS: eBook and Audiobook

SUBJECTS: Personal Challenges/ Women's Lives/Family (Fiction)

"Hood's sensitive depiction of her characters hopes and fears makes for a moving story of dedication, forgiveness, and love." —**Publishers Weekly**

"Hood's moving novel . . . ends with a pleasing sense that the red thread is more than a myth." —**Kirkus Review**

"An altogether entertaining read." —**Booklist**

"The Red Thread *is a work of aching beauty and indelible grace. A novel that elicits nothing less than wonder."* —**Dennis Lehane**

SUMMARY: *The Red Thread* is the story of six couples adopting babies from China. It is also the story of Maya, who runs the adoption agency after losing her baby daughter. And it is the story of six women in China who are forced to give up the baby girls they love. The Chinese legend of the red thread is that our children are connected to us by an invisible red thread. No matter how tangled or frayed it becomes, our child is waiting for us at the other end. Who is at the end of your red thread? Maya asks each couple.

ABOUT THE AUTHOR: **Ann Hood** is the author of ten books, including *An Ornithologist's Guide to Life*, *The Knitting Circle, Comfort*, and *The Red Thread*. Her work has appeared in *The Paris Review, Tin House, O, The Oprah Magazine*, and elsewhere. She lives in Providence, Rhode Island.

CONVERSATION STARTERS

1. Describe how each of the characters reacts to the idea of adoption. How are they similar? What makes them different?

2. How does Maya deal with the loss of her daughter? How does her reaction affect her relationships with and opinions of others?

3. How does Maya's confession to Jack change her interactions with the people around her, particularly her coworkers?

4. Flowers are a prominent motif throughout *The Red Thread*. Discuss the significance of this.

5. Many of the characters have habits that help them cope through tough situations. How do these habits help or hinder them?

6. Compare and contrast the American couples to their Chinese counterparts.

7. A red thread is said to connect mother to child. Do you think there is also a connection between the expectant mothers at the Red Thread Adoption Agency?

8. What do you think about Brooke's decision? How do you think this decision will affect her in the future? Does it change the way you view the rest of the characters?

9. Compare and contrast the babies' Chinese names and their new American ones. How do the names fulfill the hopes and dreams of the mothers, both Chinese and American?

10. How do you think the new parents will deal with the ethnic differences between themselves and their children? What types of things should they do to integrate themselves with their child's Chinese heritage?

11. What do you think will happen to each of the couples after the novel ends?

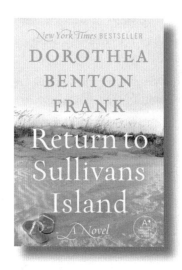

RETURN TO SULLIVANS ISLAND

AUTHOR: *Dorothea Benton Frank*

PUBLISHER: Avon A, 2010

WEBSITE: www.harpercollins.com
www.dotfrank.com

AVAILABLE IN: Trade Paperback
416 pages, $13.99, ISBN 978-0061988332

ALSO AVAILABLE AS: eBook and Audiobook

SUBJECTS: Family/Relationships/
Social Issues (Fiction)

"Tight storytelling, winsomely oddball characters and touches of Southern magic make this a winner." —**Publishers Weekly**

SUMMARY: Dorothea Benton Frank returns to the enchanted landscape of South Carolina's Lowcountry made famous in her beloved *New York Times* bestseller *Sullivans Island* to tell the story of the next generation of Hamiltons and Hayes.

Whether you were away from the Lowcountry for a week or for years, it was impossible to remember how gorgeous it was. It never changed and everyone depended on that.

Newly graduated from college and an aspiring writer, Beth Hayes craves independence and has a world to conquer. But her notions of travel, graduate study, and writing the great American novel will have to be postponed. With her mother, Susan, leaving to fulfill her own dreams in Paris and her Aunt Maggie, Uncle Grant, and stepfather, Simon, moving to California, Beth is elected by her elders to house-sit the Island Gamble. Surrounded by the shimmering blue waters of the Atlantic, the white clapboards, silver tin roof, and confessional porch have seen and heard the stories of generations of Hamiltons. But will the ghosts of the Island Gamble be watching over Beth?

ABOUT THE AUTHOR: *New York Times* bestselling author **Dorothea Benton Frank** was born and raised on Sullivans Island, South Carolina. She and her husband, Peter, divide their time between the New York area and South Carolina.

CONVERSATION STARTERS

1. When she returns from college in Boston, Beth remarks on how Sullivans Island has changed. Has your own hometown changed? If so, how? How do you feel about those changes?

2. Beth also muses about her family: "The last four years had prepared her to live her own life, independent of her tribe. Isn't that why she went to college a thousand miles away in the first place?" Is that the purpose of college? Is Beth more or less independent by the story's end?

3. Describe Beth's relationship with the women in her life: her mother, Susan, her aunts Maggie and Sophie, her friend Cecily, even her editor Barbara Farlie, their importance to her and how they shape her.

4. Determined to do her duty to the family, Beth's "intention was to avoid any and all controversy and every kind of chaos." Why does it seem that the best of intentions often go awry?

5. Beth was long wary of intimacy with men. "In her mind there was nothing more dangerous that what her mother called love." How does this mindset affect her when she meets Max Mitchell? Discuss Beth's affair with him. Why is she attracted to him?

6. What does Beth think about Woody Morrison? How do her relationships with Max and Woody contrast? What does each man offer her?

7. Beth and Susan both lost their fathers at a young age. How does this loss color different aspects of their lives?

8. Susan had always dreamed of living in Paris, but circumstances cut her stay short. Yet Susan isn't disappointed. Why? Is it always better to realize our dreams? Is there a benefit in leaving some unfilled?

9. One of the charms of the Island Gamble is that it is haunted. Do you believe in ghosts? Have you had any interesting experiences with the supernatural?

10. The author touches on the subject of race with grace and compassion. As Beth enjoys her close friendship with Cecily she thinks of the strictures placed upon her mother and Cecily's grandmother, Livvie. How else have changing social mores freed us over the years?

11. Family, independence, love, marriage, race, heartbreak, acceptance, trust, and change, are all themes interwoven in the novel. Using examples from the book, explain the role of each and how they evolve in the story's arc.

RUSSIAN WINTER

AUTHOR: *Daphne Kalotay*

PUBLISHER: HarperCollins Publishers, 2010

WEBSITE: www.harpercollins.com
www.daphnekalotay.com

AVAILABLE IN: Hardcover
480 pages, $25.99, ISBN 978-0061962165

ALSO AVAILABLE AS: eBook and Audiobook

SUBJECTS: Relationships/Art
Culture & World Issues (Fiction)

"A captivating and entertaining read." —**Oscar Hijuelos, Pulitzer Prize-winning author of** *The Mambo Kings Play Songs of Love*

"Tender, passionate, and moving." —**Jenna Blum,** *New York Times* **bestselling author of** *Those Who Save Us*

"An auspicious first novel, elegantly written and without a false note." —*Kirkus Reviews (starred review)*

SUMMARY: A mysterious jewel holds the key to a life-changing secret, in this breathtaking tale of love and art, betrayal and redemption.

Artfully interweaving past and present, Stalinist Russia and modern day New England, the behind-the-scenes tumult of theatre life and the transformative power of art, Daphne Kalotay's luminous debut novel, an ingeniously plotted page turner of the highest literary order, captures the joy, uncertainty, and terror of lives powerless to withstand the forces of history, while affirming that even in the presence of evil, suspicion, and fear the human spirit reaches for transcendence and love.

ABOUT THE AUTHOR: Author of the acclaimed fiction collection *Calamity and Other Stories*, **Daphne Kalotay** attended Boston University's Creative Writing Program before going on to complete a literature PhD. She has taught creative writing at Boston University, Middlebury College, and Skidmore College, and lives in the Boston area.

CONVERSATION STARTERS

1. How would you describe Nina Revskaya? What kind a person was she? Do you sympathize with the way events shaped the woman she became? And how would you compare her with Vera Borodina? What exactly was the nature of their friendship? What held them back from sharing their deepest secrets?

2. How does living in a repressive society like Stalin's Soviet Union affect human relationships? Can real trust ever be formed between friends, spouses, colleagues? What risks do people face in revealing their true nature?

3. Each piece of Nina's jewelry denotes a particular memory. Why do you think she waited so long to finally part with her jewels? Are there memories we have that are too painful to face, yet too dear to let go of? Do any of your possessions hold a special memory for you?

4. In your opinion, did Viktor Elsin truly love Nina? Did she love him? What about Gersh and Vera? What sacrifices were each willing to make for love?

5. After she defected, Nina believed she had shed the first third of her life. To what extent was this true? Can we ever truly rid ourselves of parts of our lives—or ourselves—that we don't like? What is the price of forgetting?

6. Themes of art, politics, and love are intertwined throughout the novel. How do art and politics influence each other? Can art be a release from political oppression? In what ways can it be oppression's tool?

7. After Nina defected to the West, she found she could not enjoy all of its freedoms. "Even when she tried to will it open, Nina's heart would not budge." Why couldn't she open herself up to new love and new friends? What held her back—habit, or guilt?

8. On their third anniversary, Viktor tells Nina, "love is all we have." But for Nina, it is dance and love. And years later, Grigori's colleague and friend Zoltan remarks, "There are only two things that really matter in life. Literature and love." Can art change the world—change who we are? Can love? Has love or a passion transformed you or someone you know?

9. Did Grigori ultimately have a better life—though it was fraught with uncertainty—because of Nina's selfishness? How might his experience have been different if he'd grown up in the Soviet Union rather than Europe and eventually America?

SADDLED
How a Spirited Horse Reined Me In and Set Me Free

AUTHOR: *Susan Richards*

PUBLISHER: Mariner Books, 2010

WEBSITE: www.marinerbooks.com
www.susan-richards.com

AVAILABLE IN: Hardcover
224 pages, $24.99, ISBN 978-0547241722

ALSO AVAILABLE AS: eBook and Audiobook

SUBJECTS: Animals/Personal Discovery/
Women's Lives (Memoir)

"*Saddled is a searingly honest portrait of addiction and the redemptive power of animal-human love.*" —**Ted Kerasote, author of *Merle's Door***

SUMMARY: One day, at the age of thirty-one, Susan Richards realized that she was an alcoholic. She wrote it down in her journal, struck by the fact that it had taken nine years of waking up hung-over to name her illness. What had changed? Susan had a new horse, a spirited Morgan named Georgia, and, as she says: "It had something to do with Georgia. It had something to do with making a commitment as enormous as caring for a horse that might live as my companion for the next forty years. It had something to do with love." Every day begins with a morning ride. Every day Susan lives a little more and thinks about her mistakes a little less.

ABOUT THE AUTHOR: **Susan Richards** has a B.A. in English from the University of Colorado and a master's degree in social work from Adelphi University. She lives with her husband Dennis Stock and their beloved gang of four dogs and one Siamese cat. She is the author of the best-selling memoir *Chosen by a Horse*.

CONVERSATION STARTERS

1. What makes Susan and Georgia a good pair? How do their differences contribute to their compatibility?

2. What attracted Susan to Stuart? What gave her the courage to leave? During the divorce, was it wise for her to ignore money and instead fight for "custody" of Georgia?

3. Now an accomplished writer, editor, and therapist, Susan has achieved much in her life. As she described her childhood struggles with school, what did you learn about a child's capacity to learn? What did her poor grades really indicate?

4. One of Susan's clearest childhood memories is of her frightful first night at her grandmother's house. In an angry outburst, Franz called Susan a prima donna. As she grew up, did affluence hurt Susan's opinion of herself? What role can wealth contribute to a family's emotional world?

5. How did caring for animals give Susan a clear sense of the world? How did horseback riding help her stay sober? Why was the cantankerous Georgia a better horse for this mission than a docile creature, like Hotshot?

6. How did life without a mother affect Susan's paths to womanhood? What parenting skills did Georgia exhibit in mothering her foal? What is the source of Susan's abundant "parenting" skills as a therapist and as a caregiver to animals?

7. Discuss your own ride through life: Where were the safe havens in your childhood? Which people tried to topple your sense of self-worth? Which beloved creatures (human or not) taught you otherwise?

8. Words and language formed one component of Susan's healing. How did it help her to have diagnoses for the disorders that had plagued her family? How did her work as an editor help her find her path as a writer?

9. How did you react when Susan revealed Tim's double life? Can you imagine what might motivate a person to be so seemingly helpful and yet so hurtful?

10. As Susan makes peace with her father, what does she discover about the nature of his lifelong suffering? How is she healed through this understanding? Why are some people able to show affection only when they are near the end of life?

11. The memoir contains many images of houses. What did it take for Susan to call a house a home, from summer camp to her own farmhouse?

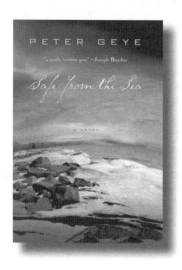

SAFE FROM THE SEA

AUTHOR: *Peter Geye*

PUBLISHER: Unbridled Books,
September 2010

WEBSITE: www.unbridledbooks.com

AVAILABLE IN: Hardcover
256 pages, $24.95, ISBN 978-1609530082

SUBJECTS: Personal Discovery/
Relationships/Family (Fiction)

"Peter Geye has rendered the Minnesota north shore in all its stark, dangerous beauty, and it is the perfect backdrop for this deeply moving story of conflict and forgiveness. Safe from the Sea *is a remarkable debut."*
—**Ron Rash**

SUMMARY: *Safe From the Sea* is the story of a man returning home to Duluth to help his ailing father. But returning home makes Noah tense and uncertain. He and his father have been estranged for years, an estrangement that began after his father survived the sinking of his Great Lakes ore boat during Noah's youth. Survived in body, but not in spirit. Once Noah arrives, though, it's clear that his father is not simply ill but dying—which the father knows, though he hasn't been explicit. He doesn't want sympathy. And so the two begin an awkward journey toward the end of Olaf Torr's life and, possibly, toward reconciliation.

ABOUT THE AUTHOR: **Peter Geye** received his MFA from the University of New Orleans and his PhD from Western Michigan University, where he was editor of *Third Coast*. He was born and raised in Minneapolis and continues to live there with his wife and three children. This is his first novel.

CONVERSATION STARTERS

1. How has grief changed the lives of the main characters in this novel?

2. How does setting affect these characters, and reflect them?

3. Did Noah make the right decision to go help his father and leave Natalie?

4. Noah is interested in ski jumping and in old maps. How do these metaphors shape the story?

5. Why do you think Olaf turned to Noah for help instead of turning to Solveig? Were his reasons deeper than the obvious?

6. How are these characters now safe from the sea?

7. Olaf presents his son with a special request. Do you think it was too much to ask? Were you surprised with how things played out?

8. Is this book about fathers and fatherhood? Or is it more a book about family?

9. Alyson Hagy, in praising the novel, said it was "All shipwreck and rescue." Do you agree? If so, how?

10. Some would argue this is a novel of redemption. Discuss.

11. Noah is ambivalent about his own possible fatherhood, given his childhood. But he recognizes the meaning a child would bring to Natalie's life. How do his wife's fertility problems and efforts complicate his emotions? In what ways does reconciliation with his father deepen his relationship with his wife and allow him to consider a fatherhood determined by who he is as a man and not who he was as a child?

SECRETS OF
THE TUDOR COURT

AUTHOR: **D. L. Bogdan**

PUBLISHER: Kensington Trade Paperback, 2010

WEBSITE: www.kensingtonbooks.com

AVAILABLE IN: Trade Paperback
352 pages, $15.00, ISBN 978-0758241993

ALSO AVAILABLE AS: eBook

SUBJECTS: History/Women's Lives/ Relationships (Fiction)

"A beautifully written story with wonderful attention to detail. I loved the book."—**Diane Haeger, author of *The Queen's Mistake***

SUMMARY: When young Mary Howard receives the news that she will be leaving her home for the grand court of King Henry VIII, to attend his mistress Anne Boleyn, she is ecstatic. Everything Anne touches seems to turn to gold, and Mary is certain Anne will one day become Queen. But Mary has also seen the King's fickle nature and how easily he discards those who were once close to him.

Discovering that she is a pawn in a carefully orchestrated plot devised by her father, the duke of Norfolk, Mary dare not disobey him. Yet despite all of her efforts to please him, she too falls prey to his cold wrath. Not until she becomes betrothed to Harry Fitzroy, the Duke of Richmond and son to King Henry VIII, does Mary finds the love and approval she's been seeking. But just when Mary believes she is finally free of her father, the tides turn. Now Mary must learn to play her part well in a dangerous chess game that could change her life—and the course of history.

ABOUT THE AUTHOR: **D.L. Bogan** is a history major, aiming for a master's so that she might lecture one day. She makes her home in central Wisconsin.

CONVERSATION STARTERS

1. Discuss how Mary's character changes throughout the novel.

2. Who were Mary's biggest influences?

3. How did Mary's regard for the king change throughout the novel?

4. Discuss Mary's fascination with Norfolk's hands.

5. How do you think Norfolk regards Mary? What were the major contributors to his persona?

6. What were, in your opinion, the three biggest turning points in the novel?

7. Analyze The Kiss.

8. Compare and contrast Mary's relationships with Harry, Cedric, and Master Foxe. Of these three, who would you consider "the love of her life"?

9. Did your opinion of Mary's mother change throughout the novel? If so, how?

10. Why do you think the novel was told in the first person, present tense? Is this a writing style you like?

11. Why does Mary refer to her father as "Norfolk" throughout the novel? How does this affect her view of him?

12. Three themes are present in the novel: self-preservation, the rainbow, and the circlet. What is the relevance of these three themes to the story? Why do you think the author chose to expound on them?

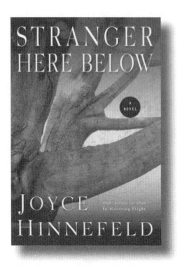

STRANGER HERE BELOW

AUTHOR: *Joyce Hinnefeld*

PUBLISHER: Unbridled Books,
October 2010

WEBSITE: www.unbridledbooks.com

AVAILABLE IN: Hardcover
288 pages, $24.95, ISBN 978-1609530044

ALSO AVAILABLE AS: eBook

SUBJECTS: Family/Women's Issues/
Relationships (Fiction)

"In her lovely new novel, Joyce Hinnefeld introduces us to a fascinating cast of characters—sisters, visitors, pilgrims, strangers—and untangles the mysteries of their lives with her distinctive grace and delicacy. She is a remarkable writer who gives her readers pleasures to savor on every page." —**Joanna Scott**

SUMMARY: In 1961, when Amazing Grace Jansen, a firecracker from Appalachia, meets Mary Elizabeth Cox, the daughter of a Black southern preacher, at Kentucky's Berea College, they already carry the scars and traces of their mothers' troubles. Poor and single, Maze's mother has had to raise her daughter alone and fight to keep a roof over their heads. Mary Elizabeth's mother has carried a shattering grief throughout her life, a loss so great that it has disabled her and isolated her stern husband and her brilliant, talented daughter. The caution this has scored into Mary Elizabeth has made her defensive and too private and limited her ambitions, despite her gifts as a musician. But Maze's earthy fearlessness might be enough to carry them both forward toward lives lived bravely in an angry world that changes by the day. Both of them are drawn to the enigmatic Georginea Ward, an aging idealist who taught at Berea sixty years ago.

ABOUT THE AUTHOR: **Joyce Hinnefeld** is an Associate Professor of Writing at Moravian College in Bethlehem, PA. Her first novel, *In Hovering Flight*, was a #1 Indie Next Pick.

CONVERSATION STARTERS

1. With whom do you most identify, Maze or Mary Elizabeth?

2. What role does faith play in this novel?

3. How does music change these girls' lives?

4. How do you feel about the portrayal of men in this novel?

5. Does this novel illuminate history for you in a new way?

6. Is this a novel about race?

7. Is this a novel about feminism?

8. Has your perception of the cover changed, having now read the book?

9. Mothers have a profound impact on the lives of their daughters in this novel. Discuss.

10. Discuss the names of the characters in the novel.

11. Are the women in this novel a family?

A STRANGER ON THE PLANET

Author: *Adam Schwartz*

Publisher: Soho Press, January 2011

Website: www.sohopress.com

Available in: Hardcover
304 pages, $24.00, ISBN 978-1569478691

Also Available as: eBook

Subjects: Family/Relationships/Identity
(Fiction)

"A stunningly good book. . . . Utterly charming." —**Don Lee, author of
Wrack and Ruin**

"Funny, honest and obsessive, A Stranger on the Planet *is finally as beautiful
as it is driven. Charming, too: Adam Schwartz is one part Philip Roth, but
with a neurosis all his own."* —**Gish Jen, author of *Typical American***

Summary: In the summer of 1969, Seth Shapiro is twelve years old, and the
personal tumult of his and his family's lives plays out against the backdrop
of the moon landing and Woodstock. Seth lives with his unstable mother,
Ruth, his twin sister, Sarah, and his younger brother, Seamus, in a two-
bedroom apartment in northern New Jersey. His father, a wealthy doctor,
lives with his young French wife in a ten-room house and has no interest in
Seth and his siblings. Seth is dying to escape from his mother's craziness
and often suffocating love for her children, her marriage to a man she's
known for two weeks, and his father's cold disregard. But over the next
four decades, as his quest for happiness and fulfillment takes him from
New Jersey to Chicago to Cambridge, Massachusetts, Seth becomes the
keeper of his family's memories and secrets. At the same time, he isolates
himself emotionally from all those who love him, especially his mother.
But Ruth is also Seth's muse, and this ultimately enables him to find
redemption, for both himself and his family.

About the Author: **Adam Schwartz** is a senior lecturer in the writing
program at Wellesley College. His stories have been widely anthologized,
and portions of *A Stranger on the Planet* have previously been published
as stories in the *New Yorker*. This is his first novel.

CONVERSATION STARTERS

1. "Do you know what your problem is?" Seth's father says to him. "You remember everything that's not important." What role does Seth's memory play in the novel? Despite his father's comments, why is Seth's capacity for remembering "everything that's unimportant" one of his most valuable and endearing qualities? Near the end of the book, Seth comments, "We'd be the happiest family in the world if no one remembered anything." But how do the stories and memories of any family define and enrich their lives? What is the role of memory and storytelling in any family's understanding of itself?

2. Seth's brother, Seamus, accuses Seth of acting funny when he's really sad. What is the role of humor in a novel with so much sadness?

3. Seth is deeply in love with his wife, Molly, but confesses to his sister that he didn't love her well enough. Why doesn't Seth do a better job of loving Molly?

4. On her deathbed, Ruth says to Seth, "I hope I was a good mother," and Seth replies, "Yes, of course you were." Does Seth believe his own words? Is Ruth a good mother? Is Seth a good son?

5. Like many children of difficult parents, Seth and Sarah are afraid of becoming like their mother. But how are both Seth and Ruth "Strangers on the Planet"?

6. The one male character Seth forms a close relationship with is Raymond, who is blind and gay. Why does Seth befriend Raymond, and why does he react so badly when he realizes that Raymond is gay?

7. In the chapter "Virgins," Rachel looses her virginity to Seth, but how does Seth loose his "virginity" as a writer? How does this experience change his life?

8. What is the relationship between the short story "A Stranger on the Planet" and the novel itself? Early in the novel, Seth says, "Nothing seemed real to me except the novels I read." Why is literature such an important medium of self-knowledge for Seth?

9. After Seth and Raymond see the movie *The Searchers*, Raymond comments: "John Wayne isolates himself from love and caring. But when he discovers Natalie Wood, he realizes his capacity for nurturing and love. She's his best half and he finally becomes a whole person." How do Raymond's words also characterize Seth? Does Seth ever become a whole person? Does he ever find his best half?

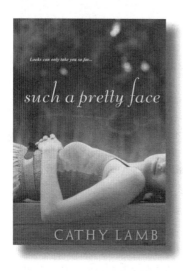

SUCH A PRETTY FACE

AUTHOR: *Cathy Lamb*

PUBLISHER: Kensington Trade Paperback, 2010

WEBSITE: www.kensingtonbooks.com
www.cathylamb.net

AVAILABLE IN: Trade Paperback
480 pages, $15.00, ISBN 978-0758229557

ALSO AVAILABLE AS: eBook

SUBJECTS: Women's Lives/
Personal Discovery/Identity (Fiction)

"Lamb delivers grace, humor and forgiveness." —**Publishers Weekly**

SUMMARY: Two years and 170 pounds ago, Stevie Barrett was wheeled into an operating room for surgery that most likely saved her life. Since that day, a new Stevie has emerged, one who walks without wheezing, plants a garden for self-therapy, and builds and paints fantastical wooden chairs. At thirty-five, Stevie is the one thing she never thought she'd be: thin.

But for everything that's changed, some things remain the same. Stevie's shyness refuses to melt away. She still can't look her neighbors' gorgeous great-nephew in the eye. The Portland law office where she works remains utterly dysfunctional, as does her family—the aunt, uncle, and cousins who took her in when she was a child. To top it off, her once supportive best friend clearly resents her weight loss. The biggest challenge in Stevie's new life is learning how to let go of all the pain—along with the pounds—while searching for love and acceptance

ABOUT THE AUTHOR: **Cathy Lamb**, the author of *Julia's Chocolates, The Last Time I Was Me*, and *Henry's Sisters*, lives in Oregon. She is married with three children. She writes late at night when it's just her and the moon and a few shooting stars.

CONVERSATION STARTERS

1. Which character in the book do you relate to, or like, the most? Do you recognize any of your own personality characteristics in Stevie, Lance, Polly, Cherie, Herbert, Crystal, Aunt Janet, Glory, Albert, or Zena?

2. What are the differences in Stevie Barrett's life pre- and post-bariatric surgery? Would you want to be friends with her? Would you have been friends with her before the operation? If yes, why; and if no, what would have prevented that friendship?

3. Discuss Helen. Did she love both her children? What would it be like to be Helen? How did the author build sympathy for her, even though she threw both daughters over a bridge?

4. What in Stevie's past brought on her obsession with chairs? What do the chairs reflect about her state of mind? If you built and painted a chair that was a reflection of you, what would it look like? If you built and painted chairs for each other, what would they look like?

5. Were Zena and Lance a good match? Would you rather date Lance or Jake? Both? Neither? Why?

6. Describe Aunt Janet and her development from the beginning of the book to the end. Do you respect her? Was she a pathetic figure or a strong one? Did she fail as a second mother to Stevie and as a mother to Lance and Polly by not leaving Herbert? Did she fail herself in staying? How so?

7. Stevie's relationship with Helen was fraught with pain, guilt, anger, blame, sorrow, embarrassment, shame, and hate, but she comes to a sort of peace with her mother by the end of the book. Was this realistic? Will Stevie ever "get over" her childhood?

8. Stevie's grandparents were in a romantic, enduring love affair with each other. How did this impact Stevie in her childhood and in her adult life? What did Stevie learn from them about life, leadership, love, compassion, heartbreak, and family?

9. There are many serious issues discussed in the book: obesity, anorexia, childhood abuse, gay marriage, divorce, self-esteem problems, death, grief, relationship issues, mental illness, and so on, but there are also humorous scenes. Did the author balance the two correctly?

10. What are the underlying themes in *Such a Pretty Face*?

11. What advice would you give Stevie for her future? What advice would she give you?

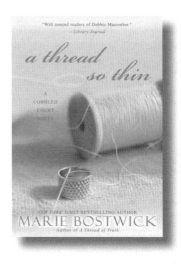

A THREAD SO THIN

AUTHOR: *Marie Bostwick*

PUBLISHER: Kensington Trade Paperback, 2010

WEBSITE: www.kensingtonbooks.com
www.mariebostwick.com

AVAILABLE IN: Trade Paperback
352 pages, $15.00, ISBN 978-0758232168

ALSO AVAILABLE AS: eBook and Audiobook

SUBJECTS: Relationships/Women's Lives/ Spirituality (Fiction)

"Bostwick's contemporary New England quilters [Cobbled Court] series is an unbreakable thread of friendship and faith." —Publishers Weekly

SUMMARY: While New Bern, Connecticut, lies under a blanket of snow, the Cobbled Court Quilt Shop remains a cozy haven for its owner, Evelyn Dixon, and her friends. Evelyn relishes winter's slower pace—besides, Internet sales are hopping, thanks to her son Garrett's efforts. In addition to helping out at the shop, Garrett has also been patiently waiting for his girlfriend, Liza, to finish art school in New York City. But as much as Evelyn loves Liza, she wonders if it's a good idea for her son to be so serious, so soon, with a young woman who's just getting ready to spread her wings.

Liza's wondering the same thing, especially after Garrett rolls out the red carpet for a super-romantic New Year's Eve—complete with marriage proposal. The only happy marriage Liza's ever seen is her aunt Abigail's, and it took her decades to tie the knot. And when she finds herself torn between a rare career opportunity and her love for Garrett, Liza must grasp at the thinnest of threads—and pray that it holds.

ABOUT THE AUTHOR: **Marie Bostwick Skinner** was born and raised in the Northwest. Marie has three handsome sons and now lives with her husband in Connecticut where she writes, reads, quilts, and is active in her local church.

CONVERSATION STARTERS

1. In Marie Bostwick's previous novel, *A Single Thread,* Evelyn Dixon is a Texas housewife, who in a matter of days must not only vacate her marriage but also her home. If the circumstances of life called for you to leave your home and move quickly, where would you go? How would you cope? What would scare you about the situation? What would excite you?

2. After only a few hours in New Bern, Evelyn realizes she feels more at ease in the New England town than she ever did in her planned suburban development. Do you believe certain places can speak to us? Can you recall a place where you immediately felt at home? Do you know why?

3. Abigail Burgess-Wynne, the matriarch of New Bern, appears to be popular, pragmatic, and in total control of her life. If she were not a wealthy woman, willing to support many local causes, do you think she would be as popular? Is her popularity only a factor of what she (and her money) can do for others? What could possibly make her so resistant to her niece's cry for help? What do we risk when we pin someone else's sins on another?

4. Why does it take Evelyn so long to realize that Charlie Donnelly is smitten with her? Do you think the challenges to her health had anything to do with her lack of awareness of his feelings? Have you ever been unaware of someone's feelings for you, and what did you do when you finally realized those feelings?

5. Three of the scariest words in the world: You have cancer. After Evelyn hears them, she breaks down not with friends but before three strangers. Why? What is the most unusual situation in your life from which you ultimately made a friend? If you have had cancer or have known someone battling cancer, what did the experience teach you? What would you share about this six-letter word?

6. Too often we believe we are loved for our breasts or our muscles, our looks or our hair, when ideally we all want to be loved for the cocktail of qualities that makes us, well, us. What are your perennial, unchanging qualities—both good and bad, quirky and mundane, silly and serious?

7. Life doesn't promise that we will always be happy, but Evelyn manages to piece together what she needs to face the journey: a group of loyal friends. Name three things that would help you through the ups and downs of life.

THE THREE WEISSMANNS OF WESTPORT

Author: *Cathleen Schine*

Publisher: Picador USA, 2010

Website: www.picadorusa.com
www.cathleenschine.com

Available in: Trade Paperback
304 pages, $14.00, ISBN 978-0312680527

Also Available as: eBook and Audiobook

Subjects: Women's Lives/Family/
Relationships (Fiction)

"Schine's real wit playfully probes the lies, self-deceptions, and honorable hearts of her characters." —**The New Yorker**

Summary: Just as Jane Austen delighted readers with wise heroines and surprising turns of fate, Cathleen Schine delivers a world of wry insight in each of her novels. With *The Three Weissmanns of Westport*, she brings *Sense and Sensibility* to modern-day Connecticut, where Betty Weissmann and her two middle-aged daughters have begun living as exiles. At age seventy-five, Betty has been dumped by her husband of nearly fifty years. He and his mistress have set up housekeeping in the sumptuous Manhattan apartment that Betty had called home for most of her adult life. Her daughter Miranda—a tough-as-nails literary agent—is facing bankruptcy after a series of scandals. Her other daughter, Annie, is smitten with the brother of her stepfather's mistress. Banding together against a slew of looming crises, Betty, Miranda, and Annie find refuge in a run-down beach cottage owned by a generous cousin. While Betty discovers a wealth of personal strength, her daughters discover an intriguing, aristocratic community— whose population includes the handsome actor Kit Maybank.

About the Author: **Cathleen Schine** is the author of *The New Yorkers* and *The Love Letter*, among other novels. She has contributed to *The New Yorker, The New York Review of Books, The New York Times Magazine*, and *The New York Times Book Review*.

CONVERSATION STARTERS

1. How do Betty and her daughters relate to men? Do the three women have the same expectations about love and relationships?

2. In *Sense and Sensibility*, Mrs. Dashwood does her best to help her family thrive despite dwindling fortunes. What challenges do women still face in such situations, even with the cultural changes that have taken place since Jane Austen was writing?

3. Which cad is worse: Schine's Kit Maybank or Austen's John Willoughby? If Miranda could meet Marianne, what advice would the two characters give each other?

4. Is Frederick a good father to Gwen and Evan? What stokes Annie's attraction to him throughout the novel?

5. Is Betty very much like her relatives? Which of your family members would you turn to if you were in her situation?

6. What accounts for the similarities and differences between Annie and Miranda? Are both women simply driven by their temperaments, or have they shaped each other's personalities throughout their lives? How does their relationship compare to yours with your own siblings?

7. Schine's work often blends humor with misfortune, such as Miranda's undoing by authors who turn out to be plagiarists and extreme fabricators. What other aspects of the novel capture the tragicomic way life unfolds?

8. Why is it so hard for Joseph to understand why his stepdaughters are mad at him? Why does he prefer Felicity to Betty? Discuss the revelations about Amber. In what way is her romantic situation similar to Felicity's?

9. Ultimately, how do the Weissmanns reconcile sense with sensibility? Who are the book's most rational characters? Who is the most emotional?

10. What makes Roberts remarkable (eventually)? Who are the overlooked "characters" in your life story?

11. What aspects of the ending surprised you the most? What had you predicted for Betty, and for Leanne? Do the novel's closing scenes reflect an Austen ending?

12. Does the storytelling style in *The Three Weissmanns of Westport* remind you of Schine's other portraits of love? What makes the Weissmanns' story unique?

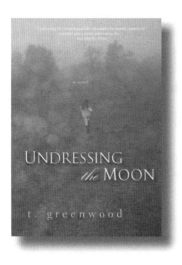

UNDRESSING THE MOON

AUTHOR: *T. Greenwood*

PUBLISHER: Kensington Trade Paperback, 2010

WEBSITE: www.kensingtonbooks.com
www.tgreenwood.com

AVAILABLE IN: Trade Paperback
288 pages, $15.00, ISBN 978-0758238764

ALSO AVAILABLE AS: eBook

SUBJECTS: Coming of Age/Women's Lives/ Personal Challenges (Fiction)

"Beautifully elucidates the human capacity to maintain grace under unrelenting fire." —**Los Angeles Times**

SUMMARY: At thirty, Piper Kincaid feels too young to be dying. Cancer has eaten away her strength; she'd be alone but for a childhood friend who's come home by chance. Yet with all the questions of her future before her, she's adrift in the past, remembering the fateful summer she turned fourteen and her life changed forever. Her nervous father's job search seemed stalled for good, as he hung around the house watching her mother's every move. What he and Piper had both dreaded at last came to pass: Her restless, artistic mother, who smelled of lilacs and showed Piper beauty, finally left. With no one to rely on, Piper struggled to hold on to what was important. She had a brother who loved her and a teacher enthralled with her potential. But her mother's absence, her father's distance, and a volatile secret threatened her delicate balance.

Now Piper is once again left with the jagged pieces of a shattered life. If she is ever going to put herself back together, she'll have to begin with the summer that broke them all.

ABOUT THE AUTHOR: **T. Greenwood** is the author of five novels, including the highly acclaimed *Two Rivers*. She lives in the Washington, D.C. area with her husband and their two daughters where she teaches creative writing, studies photography, and continues to write.

CONVERSATION STARTERS

1. Early in *Undressing the Moon*, Piper calls herself "a thirty year old girl." What caused her to see herself that way? Did she ever become a woman?

2. Piper's mother left when Piper was fourteen years old, but in a way, so did her father. Do you think she was affected more or less by his absence than her mother's? Discuss Piper's relationship with her father before and after her mother left as well as in the present.

3. Discuss Piper's relationships with all of the men in her life: her father, Quinn, Mr. Hammer, Blue Henderson, Jake. How has each of them shaped her as a woman, sexually, physically, and emotionally? Are any or all of them the reason she's single now?

4. How does Piper cope with her breast cancer? Do you think it's a healthy way to handle her illness? Do you agree with Becca when she says that Piper isn't trying to stay alive anymore? Why?

5. Piper relies on Becca for emotional strength throughout the novel, both as a teenager and as an adult. How would she have gotten through both periods of her life without Becca? What does Becca give up by helping Piper? What does she gain?

6. The image of glass—broken glass and the stained glass Piper's mother creates—is prevalent in *Undressing the Moon*. What does it represent, beyond the shattering of Piper's life? How does it relate to her current situation? Are there other images that resonate with you? If so, which ones and why?

7. Why do you think Piper blamed Mr. Hammer when Jake was the one who really raped her? In the end, was telling Quinn the truth atonement enough for that lie? Talk about Piper's breast cancer as a symbol or manifestation of the guilt she's carried.

8. What is the significance of the widow for whom Piper is making a wedding dress? What does Piper learn from her?

9. Why do you think Piper didn't ultimately go looking for her mother once she found out where she lived? Would you have sought her out if you were in that position? Should Piper have let her back into her life when she attempted to make contact?

10. What do you think happens to Piper after the book ends?

THE UNEXPECTED SON

AUTHOR: *Shobhan Bantwal*

PUBLISHER: Kensington Trade Paperback, 2010

WEBSITE: www.kensingtonbooks.com
www.shobhanbantwal.com

AVAILABLE IN: Trade Paperback
336 pages, $15.00, ISBN 978-0758232038

ALSO AVAILABLE AS: eBook

SUBJECTS: Women's Lives/Social Issues/ Personal Challenges/ (Fiction)

"Incredibly entertaining, but also enlightening." —**Harriet Klausner**

SUMMARY: It is a morning like any other in suburban New Jersey when Vinita Patil opens the battered envelope postmarked "Mumbai." But the letter inside turns her comfortable world upside down. It tells Vinita an impossible story: she has a grown son in India whose life may depend on her.

Once upon a time, a naïve young college girl fell for a wealthy boy whose primary interests were cricket and womanizing. Vinita knew, even then, that a secret affair with a man whose language and values were different from her own was a mistake. He finished with her soon enough—leaving her to birth a baby that was stillborn. Or so Vinita was told.

Now, that child is a grown man in desperate need. To help her son, to know him, Vinita must revisit her darkest hours by returning to her battle-scarred homeland—and pray for the faith of the family she leaves behind...

ABOUT THE AUTHOR: **Shobhan Bantwal** was born and raised in India and came to the United States as a young bride in an arranged marriage. She has published short fiction in literary magazines and articles in a number of publications. Writing plays in her mother tongue (Indian language— Konkani) and performing on stage at Indian-American conventions are some of her hobbies. She lives in New Jersey with her husband.

CONVERSATION STARTERS

1. In a close-knit, conservative society like Palgaum's in the 1970s, what were the chances of a girl like Vinita and a man like Som marrying? Would their marriage survive?

2. Why does Vinita's family lie to her about her child dying? As heartless as it seems, are their actions justified?

3. If Vinita had been awake during childbirth and had insisted on keeping the child, what kind of a twist would it lend to the story?

4. Is Girish's reaction to Vinita's confession too strong? Unexpected? If so, why?

5. Why doesn't Vinita automatically think of her brother or mother as prospective bone marrow donors when she's told she can't be one?

6. Is Rohit's reaction to Vinita's sudden appearance appropriate under the circumstances? Discuss the issue of an adopted child and biological parent meeting for the first time.

7. A remotely possible but unlikely marrow donor is Som Kori's wife (since she's his first cousin). Discuss the implications of that particular scenario.

8. Why are Vishal and Sayee's twin sons referred to a few times, but never appear in the book? What role do they play?

9. Vinita's mother is almost always harsh in her judgment of Vinita. Is she justified in her attitude?

10. Discuss Arya's role in the story. What does she bring to the plot?

11. Vishal is always the stern, humorless brother. What motivates him in his relationship with Vinita? Discuss his behavior and what it means to you as a reader.

12. Discuss some other ways the story could have ended. Get as creative as you wish.

UP FROM THE BLUE

AUTHOR: *Susan Henderson*

PUBLISHER: Harper Paperbacks, 2010

WEBSITE: www.litpark.com
www.harpercollins.com

AVAILABLE IN: Trade Paperback
336 pages, $13.99, ISBN 978-0061984037

ALSO AVAILABLE AS: eBook

SUBJECTS: Coming of Age/Social Issues/
Women's Lives (Fiction)

"A haunting tale of the terrible ways in which we fail each other; of the whys, the what ifs, and the what nows. This is not a book you'll soon forget." — **Sara Gruen, *New York Times* bestselling author of *Water for Elephants***

SUMMARY: When Tillie Harris goes into labor with her first child, nothing is right. Her husband is away on business, the boxes in her new home aren't unpacked, and the telephone isn't even connected yet. Forced to reach out to her estranged father for help, Tillie must face the painful memories she's been running from since she was a little girl – the memories of her own mother and the year that changed *everything*.

ABOUT THE AUTHOR: **Susan Henderson** is a two-time Pushcart Prize nominee and the founder of the literary blog LitPark: Where Writers Come to Play (www.litpark.com). She is the curator of NPR's DimeStories, and is the recipient of an Academy of American Poets award. Her work has appeared in *Zoetrope, Pittsburgh Quarterly, North Atlantic Review, Opium, Other Voices, Amazon Shorts, The Future Dictionary of America, The Best American Nonrequired Reading*, and *Not Quite What I Was Planning*. Henderson lives in New York. *Up from the Blue* is her first novel.

CONVERSATION STARTERS

1. *Up From the Blue* features a frame story (a story within a story). How do the chapters about grown Tillie enrich the story of 8-year-old Tillie? How would the novel be different if the author had only written about young Tillie?

2. Eight-year-old Tillie is introduced as a biter who liked to leave a mark. What was your initial impression of her? What do you think she craved?

3. Describe the difference between how Phil and Tillie experienced the same events. Which character was more sympathetic to you? Does it surprise you that the same events could impact siblings so differently?

4. Do you think it's realistic that no one knew what was happening inside the Harris family's home? Why do you suppose Phil and Tillie didn't tell a neighbor or a teacher?

5. Throughout the novel, Tillie made references to the neighbors who seemed to live such peaceful lives, but through her contact with the other children, she became aware of divorce, bullying, and racism. In what way is it helpful to see Tillie's situation in the context of the larger community?

6. What did you learn about Tillie by the people she's drawn to and how close she allows herself to get to them?

7. When Tillie discovered her mother in the secret room, did you believe what was happening?

8. Were you surprised to learn why Mara disappeared? And were you frustrated with the characters for their actions or inactions?

9. By the end of the story, Tillie seemed more open to reconnecting with her father, while Phil had gone his own way. What would you have done?

10. How did you find the final scene between grown Tillie and her father? What was your reaction to Tillie's statement, "I want him to be as powerful a father as he is a scientist"?

11. By the end of the story, Tillie seemed more open to reconnecting with her father, while Phil had gone his own way. What would you have done?

12. In the closing chapter, Tillie wonders what her mother might have become if they'd offered her help? Do you think she could have been helped?

13. What kind of mother do you think Tillie will be? What makes you feel hopeful or pessimistic about her future? Do you think children from unstable upbringings struggle about starting families of their own?

14. What does the title mean to you?

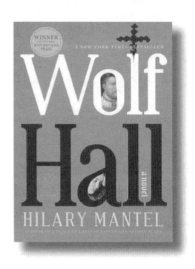

WOLF HALL

AUTHOR: *Hilary Mantel*

PUBLISHER: Picador USA, 2010

WEBSITE: www.picadorusa.com

AVAILABLE IN: Trade Paperback
640 pages, $16.00, ISBN 978-0312429980

ALSO AVAILABLE AS: eBook and Audiobook

SUBJECTS: History/Religion/
Culture & World Issues (Fiction)

**2009 Man Booker Prize Winner
2009 National Book Critics Circle Award Winner**

"The story of Cromwell's rise shimmers in Ms. Mantel's spry intelligent prose . . . [Mantel] leaches out the bones of the story as it is traditionally known, and presents to us a phantasmagoric extravaganza of the characters' plans and ploys, toils and tactics." —**Washington Times**

SUMMARY: England in the 1520s is a heartbeat from disaster. If the king dies without a male heir, the country could be destroyed by civil war. Henry VIII wants to annul his marriage of twenty years, and marry Anne Boleyn. The pope and most of Europe opposes him. The quest for the king's freedom destroys his adviser, the brilliant Cardinal Wolsey, and leaves a power vacuum.

Into this impasse steps Thomas Cromwell. Cromwell is a wholly original man, a charmer and a bully, both idealist and opportunist, astute in reading people and a demon of energy: he is also a consummate politician, hardened by his personal losses, implacable in his ambition. But Henry is volatile: one day tender, one day murderous. Cromwell helps him break the opposition, but what will be the price of his triumph?

ABOUT THE AUTHOR: **Hilary Mantel** is the author of ten novels, and the memoir, *Giving Up the Ghost*, winner of the 2006 Hawthornden Prize. All her books are available from Picador and Henry Holt. Her reviews and essays appear in T*he New York Times*, *The New York Review of Books*, and the *London Review of Books*.

CONVERSATION STARTERS

1. What is the significance of Mantel's "occult" history of Britain? How might these legendary traditions have influenced Henry in choosing to marry Anne Boleyn? What role does legend play in the perpetuation of a monarchy?

2. Why was Cromwell so attached to Cardinal Wolsey? Was Wolsey more of a mentor or a father-figure for Cromwell? What do love and loyalty mean for Cromwell?

3. Why is it meant as an insult when Norfolk calls Cromwell a "person?" What is it about Cromwell that frustrates members of the nobility so much? Why were Wolsey and Henry able to appreciate Cromwell's talents when everyone else merely saw him as an impudent schemer?

4. What is it that makes Cromwell resolve to be gentle and mild with his children? What gave him the will and the confidence to become a different man than his father?

5. What kind of a character is Thomas More in this novel? Does he come off as sympathetic in any way? Why does More choose to die rather than accept breaking away from the Catholic Church? Would Cromwell be willing to die for his beliefs?

6. What kind of a king is Henry VIII in this novel? What motivates him? Are his preoccupations solely self-interested, or does he have the good of the country in mind as well? What is it that makes him so susceptible to Anne Boleyn's seductions?

7. In conjuring Cromwell on the page, what does Mantel create, and what does she re-create from this historical record? Along those lines, how does historical fiction influence the way we look at history?

8. What is the significance of Guido Camillo's "memory machine?" Why is Cromwell interested in it? Does he see it as some sort of potential weapon, or is he driven by a desire for knowledge?

9. Is there something tragic about the fate of Elizabeth Barton the prophetess? Was she merely deceived by the monks, or was there something cynical about her? Did it seem that she ever believed in her visions? If she had not been exploited for political gain, might she have made a genuine contribution to spiritual life at the time? Or was she simply a fraud?

10. Is there any indication in the portrayal of Jane Seymour in *Wolf Hall* of the role she would later play? What might motivate Seymour to foster high ambitions? How might Seymour be similar to Cromwell?

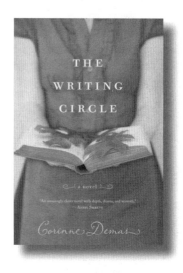

THE WRITING CIRCLE

AUTHOR: *Corinne Demas*

PUBLISHER: Voice, 2010

WEBSITE: www.everywomansvoice.com
www.corinnedemas.com

AVAILABLE IN: Hardcover
304 pages, $23.99, ISBN 978-1401341145

ALSO AVAILABLE AS: eBook

SUBJECTS: Personal Challenges/
Relationships/Women's Lives (Fiction)

"Through its artful use of multiple voices, its memorable characters and elegant prose, The Writing Circle *weaves a web that tightens slowly around you as you read until you find you simply can't put it down. This is a wonderful book, tense, engaging, and highly recommended."*
—Karen Joy Fowler, author of *The Jane Austen Book Club*

SUMMARY: When Nancy, whose most recently published work is a medical newsletter, is asked to join a writing group made up of established writers, she accepts, warily. She's not at all certain that her novel is good enough for the company she'll be keeping. Her novel is a subject very close to her heart, and she isn't sure she wants to share it with others, let alone the world. But Nancy soon finds herself as caught up in the group's personal lives as she is with their writing. She learns that nothing—love, family, loyalty—is sacred or certain.

ABOUT THE AUTHOR: **Corinne Demas** is the author of *Eleven Stories High: Growing Up in Stuyvesant Town, 1948–1968*, a memoir; two collections of short stories; a collection of poems; and numerous books for children. She has been the recipient of two National Endowment for the Arts Creative Writing Fellowships as well as an Andrew W. Mellon Fellowship. She divides her time between Western Massachusetts and Cape Cod. She has belonged to several writing circles.

CONVERSATION STARTERS

1. What did you think of the novel's structure? What were the benefits of receiving the story via alternating chapters from the perspectives of several characters? What were some of the drawbacks?

2. One of the novel's main subjects is fidelity. Discuss what Demas is saying about fidelity via her characters and their actions—not just concerning sexual relationships, but with regard to friends, family, peers, and one's sense of self. In particular, examine the lives of the members of the Leopardi Circle and the role fidelity plays in each of their lives.

3. Discuss jealousy as a subject of the novel, and the comment Demas is making about the nature of jealousy in our lives. How many kinds of jealousy are in evidence here? Is there any jealousy that might be considered healthy?

4. Which character or characters appealed to you the most, and why? Whose perspective did you sympathize or identify with the least?

5. Would you label Gillian a sociopath? Consider her behavior throughout the novel—is she consistently self-serving and remorseless? Does she have any redeeming qualities? In particular, discuss the last chapter, when it's revealed that she doesn't love anyone, but that she believes she came closest to loving Paul. Is there any irony in a poet being an amoral person?

6. Compare and contrast, too, the various partnerships in the novel: Gillian and Jerry; Rachel and Paul; Virginia and Bernard; Gillian and Adam; Aimee and Bernard; Nancy and Oates; Nancy and Chris; and Nancy and Adam. Discuss each relationship and what Demas may be saying about the nature of partnerships via these characters.

7. Fatherhood is another important subject in the novel. Compare and contrast Chris's actions and attitude toward being a father with Bernard's, who becomes a father again very late in life. Discuss both men in light of Nancy's father, who is held up as a superior example. What does this novel reveal about men and their roles in the lives of their children?

8. Were you surprised to discover that Gillian had plagiarized Nancy's novel? Do you believe Gillian truly didn't think she had stolen Nancy's work? What was your reaction when you learned that Gillian had slept with the professor who accused her of plagiarizing her senior thesis?

9. Similarly, did the end of the book surprise you? What parts of the book, aside from the preface, point to this conclusion? Was the ending a satisfying resolution to the novel?

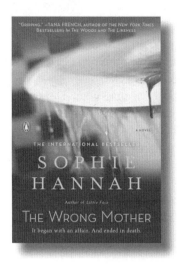

THE WRONG MOTHER

Author: *Sophie Hannah*

Publisher: Penguin Books, 2009

Website: www.penguingroup.com
www.sophiehannah.com

Available in: Trade Paperback
432 pages, $15.00, ISBN 978-0143116301

Also Available as: eBook and Audiobook

Subjects: Family/Relationships/Mystery (Fiction)

"[The Wrong Mother] is [Hannah's] most accomplished novel yet. As the revelations tumble forth, the tension is screwed ever tighter until the final shocking outcome. Exemplary." —**Daily Express (UK)**

"A superior psychological mystery. . . . Paced like a ticking time bomb with flawlessly distinct characterization, this is a fiercely fresh and un-put-downable read." —**Publishers Weekly (starred)**

Summary: Sally Thorning is watching the news with her husband when she hears an unexpected name—Mark Bretherick. It's a name she shouldn't know, but last year Sally treated herself to a secret vacation—away from her hectic family life—and met a man. After their brief affair, the two planned to never meet again. But now, Mark's wife and daughter are dead—and the safety of Sally's own family is in doubt. Sophie Hannah established herself as a new master of psychological suspense with her previous novel, *Little Face*. Now with accomplished prose and a plot guaranteed to keep readers guessing, *The Wrong Mother* is Hannah's most captivating work yet.

About the Author: **Sophie Hannah** is an internationally bestselling novelist, as well as an award-winning poet. Her other novels include *The Dead Lie Down*, *Litte Face*, and the *Truth Teller's Lie*. Her story "The Octopus Nest" won first prize in the Daphne du Maurier Festival short story competition. She lives in Yorkshire, England, with her husband and two children.

CONVERSATION STARTERS

1. Who is the "wrong mother" referred to in the novel's title?

2. Which character in the novel did you most identify with and why?

3. Why is it important to voice the negative aspects of parenthood as well as the positive?

4. Did Sally and Nick do the right thing by selling the home they loved to move somewhere they hated in order to allow their children to attend a good school? Is that kind of sacrifice something that ultimately hurts or benefits a child?

5. Would Sally have been tempted to have an affair if she and Nick had remained childless? Should she confess her infidelity to Nick?

6. It is ironic that Sally's job involves preserving Venice from sinking into the sea when she herself is barely able to keep emotionally afloat. Are there any other instances in which the author employs metaphor to illustrate a point?

7. What is Pam Senior's role in the novel?

8. Should mothers be able to take vacations from mothering?

9. Did Encarna invite her own fate? Consider the lengths to which Jon went to protect his daughter's good name: was he merely driven insane by their deaths, or was he trying to do something honorable?

10. Cordy is the only character whose family remains unscathed by the madness that unfolds around her. Is it her selfishness or just luck that ultimately preserves Oonagh?

11. If it is at all possible to compare two unspeakable horrors, which crime is worse—a mother who kills a child or a child who kills his or her mother?

12. Is Amy's chronic lying evidence of her unhappiness at home? If so, to what would you attribute Lucy's ruthless honesty? Do parents generally accept too much blame for their children's unsavory attributes or not enough?

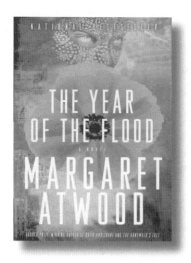

THE YEAR OF THE FLOOD

AUTHOR: *Margaret Atwood*

PUBLISHER: Anchor Books, 2010

WEBSITE: www.ReadingGroupCenter.com
www.yearoftheflood.com

AVAILABLE IN: Trade Paperback
448 pages, $15.00, ISBN 978-0307455475

ALSO AVAILABLE AS: eBook and Audiobook

SUBJECTS: Intrigue/Relationships/
Fantasy (Fiction)

"Written with energy, inventiveness, and narrative panache. . . . A gripping and visceral book that showcases Atwood's pure storytelling talents."
—**Michiko Kakutani,** *The New York Times*

"Enthralling. . . . Memorable characters, a tightly controlled pace, and shockingly plausible scenes make it fly—to a mysterious skin-prickling ending." —*San Francisco Chronicle*

SUMMARY: Set in the visionary future of Atwood's acclaimed *Oryx and Crake*, *The Year of the Flood* is at once a moving tale of lasting friendship and a landmark work of speculative fiction. In this second book of the MaddAddam trilogy, the long-feared waterless flood has occurred, altering Earth as we know it and obliterating most human life. Among the survivors are Ren, a young trapeze dancer locked inside the high-end sex club Scales and Tails, and Toby, who is barricaded inside a luxurious spa. Amid shadowy, corrupt ruling powers and new, gene-spliced life forms, Ren and Toby will have to decide on their next move, but they can't stay locked away.

ABOUT THE AUTHOR: **Margaret Atwood**, whose work has been published in over thirty-five countries, is the author of more than forty books of fiction, poetry, and critical essays. In addition to *The Handmaid's Tale*, her novels include *Cat's Eye*, shortlisted for the Booker Prize; *Alias Grace*, which won the Giller Prize in Canada and the Premio Mondello in Italy; *The Blind Assassin*, winner of the 2000 Booker Prize; and her most recent, *Oryx and Crake*, shortlisted for the 2003 Booker Prize. She lives in Toronto with writer Graeme Gibson.

CONVERSATION STARTERS

1. How does the friendship between Amanda and Ren grow, despite their differences and the restrictions they face? They meet as children. Who was your greatest ally when you were that age? What do you think of Ren's treatment of Bernice?

2. What survival skills do the novel's female characters possess? Do they find security or vulnerability at Scales and Tales, the AnooYoo Spa, and within the community of Gardeners? What strength does Pilar find in nature, while Lucerne is drawn to artificial beauty?

3. How do Adam One's motivations compare to Zeb's? In their world, what advantages do men have? Are they really "advantages"?

4. Discuss Toby's parents and their fate. What does their story illustrate about the dangers of an unregulated and corrupt drug industry? What motivates Toby to become a healer?

5. How does Adam One's explanation of creation and the fall of humanity compare to more standard Judeo-Christian ideas? What does he offer his followers, beyond an understanding of the planet and the creatures that inhabit it?

6. As a refugee from Texas, Amanda is an outsider, facing constant risk. Would you have harbored her? Why is Ren so impressed by her?

7. What is the result of a penal system like Painball? How does it influence the citizens' attitude toward crime?

8. Should Toby have honored Pilar's deathbed wish that she become an Eve? How did the lessons in beekeeping serve Toby in other ways as well?

9. Crake's BlyssPlus pill offers many false promises. What are they, and what was Crake really striving for (chapter 73)? If human beings are the greatest problem for the natural world, could they also provide solutions less drastic than Crake's? How?

10. In what ways do the novel's three voices—Toby's, Ren's, and Adam One's—complement one another? What unique perspective is offered in each narration?

11. Explore the lyrics from The God's Gardeners Oral Hymnbook. What do they say about the Gardener theology and the nature of their faith? Adam One does not always tell the truth to his congregation. Is well-meant lying ever acceptable?

12. Margaret Atwood's fiction often displays "gallows humor." Can a thing be dire and funny at the same time? Must we laugh or die?

13. What parallels did you see between *The Year of the Flood* and current headlines?

ZEITOUN

AUTHOR: *Dave Eggers*

PUBLISHER: Vintage Books, 2010

WEBSITE: www.ReadingGroupCenter.com

AVAILABLE IN: Trade Paperback
368 pages, $15.95, ISBN 978-0307387943

ALSO AVAILABLE AS: eBook

SUBJECTS: Social Issues/Culture &
World Issues/Family (Nonfiction)

"The stuff of great narrative nonfiction. . . . Fifty years from now, when people want to know what happened to this once-great city [New Orleans] during a shameful episode of our history, they will still be talking about a family named Zeitoun." —**Timothy Egan, The New York Times Book Review**

"A major achievement and [Eggers's] best book yet." —**The Miami Herald**

SUMMARY: Abdulrahman Zeitoun is a Syrian-born entrepreneur who runs a busy painting company in New Orleans. He is a devout Muslim, married to a native of Baton Rouge who had converted to Islam before meeting Zeitoun. As Hurricane Katrina barrels toward New Orleans, he safely evacuated his family. Abdulrahman stays behind to help neighbors battle the devastating storm. As the National Guard enter the city, armed with machine guns and surveillance helicopters, things begin to go very wrong for Abdulrahman. He is taken into custody and subject to strip searches, and even denied the right to phone his wife. Zeitoun's ordeal is the main subject of this harrowing nonfiction book, while Eggers enriches the shocking tale of injustice with a richly layered account of Zeitoun's early life on the coast of Syria, his large and loving family, his relationships with his friends, employees, and neighbors.

ABOUT THE AUTHOR: **Dave Eggers** is the author of six previous books, including *What Is the What*, a finalist for the 2006 National Book Critics Circle Award. He is the founder and editor of McSweeney's, an independent publishing house, and with Nívine Calegari he cofounded 826 Valencia, a nonprofit writing and tutoring center for youth in the Mission District of San Francisco..

CONVERSATION STARTERS

1. "Notes About This Book" (xv) gives a sense of how the book was written, whose point of view it reflects, and Eggers's efforts at accuracy and truth in his depiction of events. By choosing to portray the response to the hurricane through its effects on one family, what kind of story (or history) does he achieve?

2. The book opens with "Friday, August 26," an expository chapter that introduces us to Zeitoun's family life and his business life, the two very interconnected. What are some of the ways in which the descriptions here draw you in as a reader, and make these people and their situation real? Why is the timeline a good structural choice for this story?

3. Do Abdulrahman, Kathy and their children make up an unusual American family, or not? How would you describe the relationship between Zeitoun and Kathy, in marriage and in business? What effect does their religion have on the way others in the community see them?

4. Why has Eggers woven into the story accounts of Zeitoun's past in Syria, his upbringing, his brother Mohammed, the champion swimmer, his brother Ahmad, and their close bond? What effect does this framework of family have on your perception of Zeitoun's character, his ethics, his behavior?

5. Discuss what happens when Zeitoun and the others are forced to get into the boat and are taken into custody. Is it clear why they are being arrested? What assumptions are made about Zeitoun and the other three men (275–87)?

6. Part IV (203–90) tells the story of Zeitoun's imprisonment. Here we learn in great detail how Zeitoun is denied the right to call Kathy, how his injured foot is not attended to, how the other men are beaten, stripped, and starved, how he prays constantly, yet loses hope. What is the impact, as you read, of this narrative?

7. Discuss Kathy's situation, and her actions once she learns where Zeitoun is. The aftermath is more difficult, and she still suffers from physical and psychological problems that seem to be the result of post-traumatic stress. What was the most traumatic part of her experience, and why (319)?

8. What is Zeitoun's feeling now about what happened? How does he move forward into the future, as expressed in the book's closing pages (322–25)?

Stressed about finishing this month's choice before the meeting? Listen while you drive, exercise, cook, or clean.

READING GROUPS ARE TALKING... ABOUT *LISTENING.*

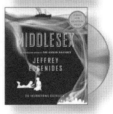

"I got all wrapped up in the story and hated when I had to stop listening. It was a nice change for the group...In fact, we had more members participate this month because it was on audio."
—Mitzi C., Lake Charles, LA

"I actually would look forward to going to work in the AM...Listening brought the characters more to life. I felt more immersed in the story."
—Peggie W., Kissimee, FL

For more information visit www.macmillanaudio.com

Become a fan of Macmillan Audio

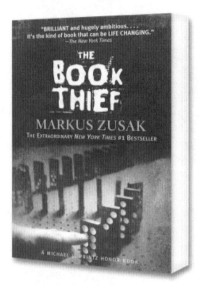
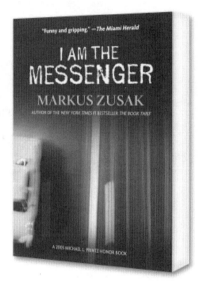

JOHN STEINBECK

Essential American Voice,
Excellent Reading Group Choice.

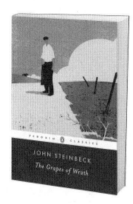 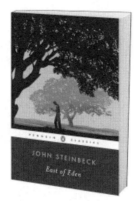 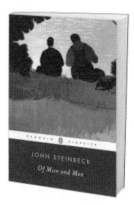

Cannery Row · *East of Eden* · *The Grapes of Wrath*
Of Mice and Men · *The Pearl* · *Sweet Thursday*
Travels with Charley in Search of America
The Winter of Our Discontent and more

For select readers guides visit penguinclassics.com

PENGUIN CLASSICS
A member of Penguin Group (USA)
www.penguin.com

VINTAGE BOOKS & ANCHOR BOOKS
Reading Group Center
THE BOOK CLUB SOURCE FOR BOOK LOVERS

Visit for the latest news on great books—award winners, bestsellers, beloved classics, movie tie-ins, and more.

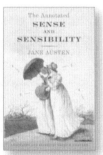
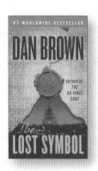

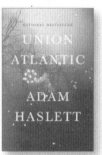

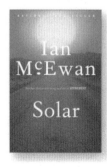

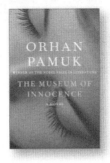 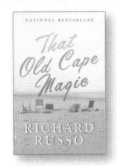 

JOIN THE DISCUSSION AT ReadingGroupCenter.com!

• **Author Chats** Conversations with favorite authors • **Discussion Guides and Tips** Almost 1,000 guides and many discussion ideas • **Group Talk** Groups nationwide share ideas, helpful tips, anecdotes, and much more—share your group's experiences • **Behind the Book Features** Author videos, original essays, and other unique and useful materials • **Reading Planner** Browse author event schedules • **And much more**

VINTAGE & ANCHOR AT THE MOVIES
First Read the Book. Then See the Movie.

There's nothing more exciting than falling in love with a book and seeing it come to life on the big screen. Browse our complete movie tie-in list online, featuring recent and upcoming releases.

• NEVER LET ME GO by Kazuo Ishiguro • PRECIOUS: based on the novel *Push* by Sapphire • THE GIRL WITH THE DRAGON TATTOO and THE GIRL WHO PLAYED WITH FIRE by Stieg Larsson

---

Sign Up for the Reading Group Center E-Newsletter And receive exclusive behind-the-scenes publishing news, author updates, special offers, and more.

Follow us on Twitter: twitter.com/RGCenter
Become a fan on Facebook: facebook.com/ReadingGroupCenter

extremely witty conversation with southern authors
most excellent recommendations for reading
clever & refined musings of booksellers & writers
engaging & amusing author readings
illuminating excerpts from great southern books
and other such items as are of interest to
her ladyship, the editor

Lady Banks' Commonplace Book
front porch literary gossip
from your favorite southern bookshops

subscribe at ladybankscommonplacebook.com

PERFECT BOOKS FOR YOUR BOOK GROUP

Family. Loyalty. Friendship. Love.

Discover Dana Reinhardt.

Remember when you
thought you knew
everything?

Remember when you
realized you didn't?

Can any lie
ever really
be harmless?

Build...
a house...
a friendship...
a family...
your life.

Can the bond between
brothers survive a war?

  DISCUSS THESE GREAT BOOKS
AT RANDOMBUZZERS.COM!

READING GROUP

We wish to thank the authors, agents, publicists, librarians, booksellers, and our publishing colleagues who have continued to support this publication by calling to our attention some quality books for group discussion, and the publishers and friends who have helped to underwrite this edition.

Algonquin Books

Anchor Books

Avon A

Bloomsbury USA

Citadel Press
Trade Paperback

Delacort Books
for Young Readers

Graywolf Press

HarperCollins Publishers

Harper Paperbacks

Harper Perennial

Houghton Mifflin Harcourt

Kensington Trade Paperback

Knopf Books
for Young Readers

Macmillian Audio

Mariner Books

Middleway Press

NAL Paperback

Other Press

Penguin Books

Picador USA

Plume/Hudson St. Press

Random House
Trade Paperbacks

Riverhead Books

Rodale

Soho Press

Southern Independent
Booksellers Alliance

Tyndale House Publishers

Unbridled Books

Vintage Books

Voice

Weiser Books

Wendy Lamb Books

William Morrow

W.W. Norton & Company

Reading Group Choices' goal is to join with publishers, bookstores, libraries, trade associations, and authors to develop resources to enhance the reading group experience.

Reading Group Choices is distributed annually to bookstores, libraries, and directly to book groups. Titles from previous issues are posted on the **www.ReadingGroupChoices.com** website. Books presented here have been recommended by book group members, librarians, booksellers, literary agents, publicists, authors, and publishers. All submissions are then reviewed to ensure the discussibility of each title. Once a title is approved for inclusion by the Advisory Board (see below), publishers are asked to underwrite production costs, so that copies of *Reading Group Choices* can be distributed for a minimal charge.

For additional copies, please call your local library or bookstore, or contact us by phone or email as shown below. Quantities are limited. For more information, please visit our website at **www.ReadingGroupChoices.com**

Toll-free: 1-866-643-6883 • info@ReadingGroupChoices.com

READING GROUP CHOICES' ADVISORY BOARD

Donna Paz Kaufman founded the bookstore training and consulting group of Paz & Associates in 1992, with the objective of creating products and services to help independent bookstores and public libraries remain viable in today's market. A few years later, she met and married **Mark Kaufman**, whose background included project management, marketing communications, and human resources. Together, they launched **Reading Group Choices** in 1994 to bring publishers, booksellers, libraries, and readers closer together. They sold **Reading Group Choices** to Barbara and Charlie Mead in May 2005. They now offer training and education for new and prospective booksellers, architectural design services for bookstores and libraries, marketing support, and a training library for professional and staff development on a wide variety of topics. To learn more about Paz & Associates, visit www.PazBookBiz.com.

John Mutter is editor-in-chief of *Shelf Awareness*, the daily e-mail newsletter focusing on books, media about books, retailing and related issues to help booksellers, librarians and others do their jobs more effectively. Before he and his business partner, Jenn Risko, founded the company in May 2005, he was executive editor of bookselling at *Publishers Weekly*. He has covered book industry issues for 25 years and written for a variety of publications, including *The Bookseller* in the U.K.; *Australian Bookseller & Publisher*; *Boersenblatt*, the German book trade magazine; and *College Store Magazine* in the U.S. For more information about *Shelf Awareness*, go to its Web site, www.shelf-awareness.com.

Mark Nichols was an independent bookseller in various locations from Maine to Connecticut from 1976 through 1993. After seven years in a variety of positions with major publishers in New York and San Francisco, he joined the American Booksellers Association in 2000, and currently serves as Senior Director, Publisher Initiatives. He is on the Board of James Patterson's ReadKiddoRead.com, and has edited two volumes with Newmarket Press—*Book Sense Best Books* (2004) and *Book Sense Best Children's Books* (2005).

Nancy Olson has owned and operated Quail Ridge Books & Music in Raleigh, NC, since 1984, which has grown from 1,200 sq. ft. to 9,000+ sq. ft and sales of $3.2 million. The bookstore won three major awards in 2001: *Publishers Weekly* Bookseller of the Year, Charles Haslam Award for Excellence in Bookselling; Pannell Award for Excellence in Children's Bookselling. It was voted "Best in the Triangle" in the *Independent Weekly* and *Metro Magazine*.

Jill A. Tardiff is publishing industry consultant and project manager working under her banner company Bamboo River Associates. She is also advertising manager for such print and online publications as *Parabola—Tradition, Myth, and the Search for Meaning*, as well as contributing editor at *Publishers Weekly*. Jill is the past president of the Women's National Book Association (WNBA) and WNBA-New York City chapter, 2004–2006 and 2000–2005, respectively. She is currently WNBA's National Reading Group Month Committee Chair and Coordinator and its United Nations Department of Public Information NGO Chief Representative. She is currently working on several book proposals on modern-day pilgrimage.

Book Group Resources

WEBSITES

About reading groups and book clubs

- **ReadingGroupChoices.com**—Over 1000 guides available plus giveaways and fun and interactive materials for reading groups.

- **bookgroupexpo.com**—Come to book group expo and celebrate.

- **Book-Clubs-Resource.com**—A guide to book clubs and reading groups with a collection of links and information for readers, including information about saving with discount book clubs.

- **BookClubCookbook.com**—Recipes and food for thought from your book club's favorite books and authors

- **bookclubgirl.com**—Dedicated to sharing great books, news, and tips with book club girls everywhere

- **bookgroupbuzz.booklistonline.com**—Book group tips, reading lists, & lively talk of literary news from the experts at Booklist Online

- **NationalReadingGroupMonth.org**—Celebrating the joy of shared reading

- **LiteraryAffairs.net**—Book club picks and author events from one of the leading book club facilitators in the country

About Books

- **ShelfAwareness.com**—A free e-mail newsletter dedicated to helping the people in stores, in libraries and on the Web buy, sell, and lend books most wisely.

- **GenerousBooks.com**—A community for those who love books and love to discuss them

- **BookMuse.com**— Commentary, author bios, and suggestions for further reading

- **BookBrowse.com**— Book reviews, excerpts, and author interviews

- **BookSpot.com**—Help in your search for the best book-related content on the Web

● **Publisher Web Sites**—Find additional topics for discussion, special offers for book groups, and other titles of interest.

Algonquin Books — **algonquin.com**

Anchor Books — **ReadingGroupCenter.com**

Avon A — **harpercollins.com**

Bloomsbury USA — **bloomsburyusa.com**

Citadel Press Trade Paperback — **kensingtonbooks.com**

Delacorte Books for Young Readers — **RandomBuzzers.com**

Graywolf Press — **graywolfpress.org**

HarperCollins Publishers — **harpercollins.com**

Harper Paperbacks — **harpercollins.com**

Harper Perennial — **harperperennial.com**

Houghton Mifflin Harcourt — **houghtonmifflinbooks.com**

Kensington Trade Paperback — **kensingtonbooks.com**

Knopf Books for Young Readers — **RandomBuzzers.com**

Macmillan Audio — **macmillanaudio.com**

Mariner Books — **marinerbooks.com**

Middleway Press — **middlewaypress.com**

NAL Paperback — **penguingroup.com**

Other Press — **otherpress.com**

Penguin Books — **penguingroup.com**

Picador USA — **picadorusa.com**

Plume/Hudson St. Press — **penguingroup.com**

Random House Trade Paperbacks — **atrandom.com**

Riverhead Books — **penguingroup.com**

Rodale — **rodale.com**

Soho Press — **sohopress.com**

Tyndale House Publishers — **tyndale.com**

Unbridled Books — **unbridledbooks.com**

Vintage Books — **ReadingGroupCenter.com**

Voice — **everywomansvoice.com**

W.W. Norton & Company — **wwnorton.com**

Weiser Books — **www.redwheelweiser.com**

Wendy Lamb Books — **RandomBuzzers.com**

William Morrow — **harpercollins.com**

BOOKS

Between the Covers: The Book Babes' Guide to a Woman's Reading Pleasures by Margo Hammond and Ellen Heltzel. De Capo Press, ISBN 978-0-7382-1229-6 $16.95

The Book Club Companion: A Comprehensive Guide to the Reading Group Experience by Diana Loevy. Berkeley Books, ISBN 0-425-21009-X, $14.00.

The Book Club Cookbook: Recipes and Food for Thought from Your Book Club's Favorite Books and Authors by Judy Gelman and Vicki Levy Krupp. Tarcher/Penguin, ISBN 1-58542-322-X, $15.95.

The Book Group Book: A Thoughtful Guide to Forming and Enjoying a Stimulating Book Discussion Group. Edited by Ellen Slezak and Margaret Eleanor Atwood. Chicago Review Press, ISBN 1-5565-2412-9, $14.95.

Book Lust: Recommended Reading for Every Mood, Moment, and Reason by Nancy Pearl. Sasquatch Books, ISBN 1-57061-381-8, $16.95.

More Book Lust: Recommended Reading for Every Mood, Moment, and Reason by Nancy Pearl. Sasquatch Books, ISBN 1-57061-435-0 $16.95.

Book Smart: Your Essential Reading List for Becoming a Literary Genius in 365 Days by Jane Mallison. McGraw Hill, ISBN 978-0-07-148271-4, $14.95

Family Book Sharing Groups: Start One in Your Neighborhood! by Marjorie R. Simic with Eleanor C. MacFarlane. The Family Literacy Center, ISBN 1-8837-9011-5, $6.95.

Good Books Lately: The One-Stop Resource for Book Groups and Other Greedy Readers by Ellen Moore and Kira Stevens. St. Martin's Griffin, ISBN 978-0-312-30961-9, $13.95.

Leave Me Alone, I'm Reading: Finding and Losing Myself in Books by Maureen Corrigan. Random House, ISBN 0-375-50425-7, $24.95.

The Mother-Daughter Book Club: How Ten Busy Mothers and Daughters Came Together to Talk, Laugh and Learn Through Their Love of Reading by Shireen Dodson and Teresa Barker. HarperCollins, ISBN 0-0609-5242-3, $14.

Running Book Discussion Groups by Lauren Zina John. Neal-Schuman, ISBN 1-55570-542-1.

The Reading Group Handbook: Everything You Need to Know to Start Your Own Book Club by Rachel Jacobsohn. Hyperion, ISBN 0-786-88324-3, $12.95.

Recipe for a Book Club: A Monthly Guide for Hosting Your Own Reading Group: Menus & Recipes, Featured Authors, Suggested Readings, and Topical Questions by Mary O'Hare and Rose Storey. Capital Books, ISBN 978-1-931-86883-9, $19.95.

Women's Fiction Authors: A Research Guide by Rebecca Vnuk. Libraries Unlimited, ISBN 978-1-591-58642-5, $40.00.

Talking About Books: Literature Discussion Groups in K–8 Classrooms by Kathy Short. Heinemann, ISBN 0-3250-0073-5, $24.

Thirteen Ways of Looking at the Novel by Jane Smiley. Knopf, ISBN 1-4000-4059-0, $26.95.

What to Read: The Essential Guide for Reading Group Members and Other Book Lovers (Revised) by Mickey Pearlman. HarperCollins, ISBN 0-0609-5313-6, $14.00.

A Year of Reading: A Month-By-Month Guide to Classics and Crowd-Pleasers for You or Your Book Group by H. E. Ellington and Jane Freimiller. Sourcebooks, ISBN 1-5707-1935-7, $14.95.

Two Great Features
on **ReadingGroupChoices.com**

MUSIC BY THE BOOK!
A pairing of music and words just for book groups!

In **MUSIC BY THE BOOK!**, Tom Moon, author of *1,000 Recordings to Hear Before You Die*, chooses different music selections that accompany book group picks.

Award-winning music journalist Tom Moon has searched out peak musical experiences from all genres and every corner of the earth. *1000 Recordings To Hear Before You Die* is the result of his journey. Covering both acknowledged world-culture masterworks and recordings that have been unfairly overlooked, the book is designed to encourage listeners to become explorers. Tom has also developed a Listening Group Guide to enhance the music lover's listening experience! Please contact Michael Rockliff to receive the Guide (mrockliff@workman.com) and visit www.1000recordings.com for more information about the joy of music.

For your next gathering, why not pair a book selection from *Reading Group Choices* with a music choice from **MUSIC BY THE BOOK!**

WINE BY THE BOOK!
A pairing of music and words just for book groups!

In **WINE BY THE BOOK!**, Laurie Forster, The Wine Coach® and author of *The Sipping Point: A Crash Course in Wine*, explores wines from regions found in book group picks.

In *The Sipping Point: A Crash Course in Wine*, Laurie gives general tips on wine essentials, including how to order wine at dinner, simplify food pairings, handle awkward wine moments, and even bounce back the morning after! Laurie's first book reflects her fresh perspective on wine education and has already received rave reviews. *The Sipping Point* won a Living Now Book Award for Cooking/Entertaining books. Please visit www.thewinecoach.com for more information about the joy of wine.

For your next gathering, why not pair a book selection from *Reading Group Choices* with a wine choice from **WINE BY THE BOOK!**

Two more *discussible ideas* to check out on
ReadingGroupChoices.com!

READING GROUPS
CHOOSE CREATIVE NAMES

Literary Epicureans
Books & Bites
Wine, Chocolate & Books
Laughter, Lunch & Literature
Coffee by the Book
Not Just Desserts
Literary Potluck
Tea and Tales

MargaReaders
Just Mai Tai'n
Book 'n Brew
Bar and a Book
Drinkers with a Reading Problem
Reading Between the Wines

B.A.G. Ladies (Books Are Good)
WOW (Women of Words)
Spine Crackers
Dewey Decimators
Bookwork Biddies
Chapter Chicks
Literal Hotties
Rabid Readers

Babel On Book Club
JUGS (Just Us Girls)
Litwits
Face2Face
Boisterous Banter
Bemused Bibliophiles
Chapter Chat
Wegab
Tattered Cover Tootsies

Praise for
Reading Group Choices

"I truly do look forward to receiving a copy of this book each year, so many great suggestions." —RENEE, TUESDAY NIGHT BOOKCLUB

"Who knew that an unexpected brown box on my doorstep could bring so much joy! When I saw the **Reading Group Choices** return address label in the upper left hand corner, I told my four kids (with absolute glee) that Mommy may have won a free book. I asked my 9 year old to bring the box inside. After considerable difficulty picking up the box I was baffled as to what could possibly be so heavy. My kids watched in wide eyed astonishment as Mommy jumped up and down clapping her hands. It turns out that my book club was chosen as a winner of **Reading Group Choices**' 15th Anniversary Drawing. The box contained not one, but *fifteen* of your selected "most discussable" books, packed neatly in a row. As it happens, our book club meeting is tomorrow. I absolutely cannot wait to show the group the box. I know the books contained inside will provide us with hours of great discussion. We will continue to use your site as an outstanding resource for book club book selection. Thank you once again for the delightful surprise!" —JODI, THE BOOK CLUB

"I sure do enjoy this website—I've written down four books I MUST READ!!" —VALERIE, THE LAST WORDSMITH

"I always look forward to your recommendations to round out our book club's choices." —PHYLLIS, GARRETT PARK TEACHERS

"**Reading Group Choices** was helpful recently when I couldn't locate a guide for *A Mighty Heart* by Marianne Pearl. A staff member searched on other sites for me, and found that one didn't exist. But they offered other helpful tips to lead discussion, and we ended up having a wonderful time. Thanks!" —SUSAN, BROADS WHO READ BOOKS

"I love **Reading Group Choices**!" —DENISE, RED BALLOONS BOOK GROUP

"**Reading Group Choices** just keeps getting better and better every month. I thought the pairing of music to books very clever . . . just wanted to extend my admiration and appreciation for a beautifully executed piece of work." —TAMBRA, UNO LADY

"Thank you for the super book list; I want to read them all!" —PHYLLIS, SATURDAY P.M. BOOK GROUP

"We give out a copy to each of our book clubs . . . They (and we) love it!" —PATRICIA, MANLIUS LIBRARY

Index by Subject Matter